TOP FIVE

TOP FIVE

HOW *HIGH FIDELITY* FOUND ITS RHYTHM AND BECAME A CULT MOVIE CLASSIC

ANDREW BUSS

APPLAUSE
THEATRE & CINEMA BOOKS

Essex, Connecticut

APPLAUSE
THEATRE & CINEMA BOOKS

An imprint of Globe Pequot, the trade division of
The Rowman & Littlefield Publishing Group, Inc.
4501 Forbes Blvd., Ste. 200
Lanham, MD 20706
www.rowman.com

Distributed by NATIONAL BOOK NETWORK

Library of Congress Cataloging-in-Publication Data

Names: Buss, Andrew, author.
Title: Top five : how High fidelity found its rhythm and became a movie
classic / Andrew Buss.
Description: Essex, Connecticut : Applause, [2023]
Identifiers: LCCN 2023010696 (print) | LCCN 2023010697 (ebook) |
ISBN 9781493072132 (paperback) | ISBN 9781493072149 (ebook)
Subjects: LCSH: High fidelity (Motion picture) | Hornby, Nick. High
fidelity—Film adaptations.
Classification: LCC PN1997.H483 B87 2023 (print) | LCC PN1997.H483
(ebook) | DDC 791.43/72—dc23/eng/20230522
LC record available at https://lccn.loc.gov/2023010696
LC ebook record available at https://lccn.loc.gov/2023010697

♾️™ The paper used in this publication meets the minimum requirements
of American National Standard for Information Sciences—Permanence of
Paper for Printed Library Materials, ANSI/NISO Z39.48-1992.

For Bill Zehme, my mentor, friend, and one of the most masterful wordsmiths journalism has ever known. This book exists thanks to your years of unmatched support and guidance.

Contents

Introduction

The key ingredient for any good story is that the audience must be able to see themselves in it. Whether it's set in the future, the past, or a world that never existed to begin with, there needs to be that big takeaway they can hone in on and proudly proclaim to all of their friends, "This is who I am."

This is something so many artists hope to achieve. Yet so few ever actually manage to do it. There are varying reasons why this is. It doesn't necessarily mean the writer isn't good at what they do. For one reason or another, their book just didn't quite connect with the audience in the way they intended it to. That's why when you have a book like *High Fidelity*, it's a triumph. Because it does all of the things it needs to do in order to connect with an audience.

Ask fifteen people what *High Fidelity* means to them and you'll almost certainly get fifteen different answers. That's because it's hard to categorize. It manages to be both a love story, while also being not your standard tale of romantic entanglement. We see the meet cute via flashback, and we see the reconciliation, but we also see the obstacles and the challenges. We see two people who realize there's certain things about the other person that they'll have to accept, because they can never successfully change one another fully.

At the beginning of *High Fidelity*, we see our protagonist Rob as he is in the midst of a rather nasty breakup with his longtime girlfriend, Laura. During the story, Rob goes back and revisits his top five heartbreaks, paying a visit to each former flame in the process. By the end of their respective journeys, he and Laura wind up back together.

But the material, smartly, leaves so much up in the air. There's no cheesy, premeditated incident that brings them closer together. Laura's relationship with Rob reignites after they hook up in the car following Laura's dad's funeral. Not the sort of thing you'd find in most love stories, is it? However, there is some truth to the point that grief brings out every sort of emotion in people, including lust and a desire to just not want to be alone anymore. The material finds the truth in those encounters.

The story also speaks to another section of people: the music and pop culture obsessive. As the owner of a record store, Rob and his loyal two-man crew do exactly what you'd imagine one would do in a record store that isn't too regularly visited: they talk about music. They also talk about movies, books, television shows, and whatever the hell else they'd fancy. Because how else are you going to kill the meaningless hours of the day when you're just waiting for something interesting to happen?

If you walked into any record store and acted as a fly on the wall for a day, it's guaranteed you'd hear many of the same discussions. However, it can almost be guaranteed that said discussions would be nowhere near as eloquently conveyed as they are by both Hornby and the film's screenwriters.

One reason why Hornby's books resonate and have stood the test of time could stem from his approach to telling these stories. They are most effective because he's able to find a balance between removing himself from the story while maintaining abstract traces of himself and the people he knew throughout.

While certain facets of the book may have semi-autobiographical undertones, at the end of the day, the novel is just that: a novel.

Hornby used himself as the light foundation, and then from there, Rob evolved into someone else entirely. Rob is his own person and not an exact reflection of Hornby.

Like Hornby's knack for drawing from real life while also turning the story into its own thing, *High Fidelity*'s director Stephen Frears has a similar gift. If you look at the incredible body of work that he's given us over the course of his career, there's an overarching theme throughout: so many of the stories he tells in his films are about the human condition.

That was his draw to the world of *High Fidelity*. It wasn't about the music, certainly. Frears will be the first to admit that their music world wasn't exactly his. However, the story that he was immediately drawn to was the love story between Rob and Laura. It was all about examining Rob and digging into who he is. Frears let everyone else worry about the music. He was much more interested in examining the human behavior of the *High Fidelity* gang.

When it comes to page-to-screen adaptations, there's a few reasons why a lot of times they are hit or miss. Sometimes they take things too literally and it feels like a jumbled mess where the screenwriters just copied and pasted everything from the book into the script. Other times, as a viewer, you find yourself wondering if the people who made the film even read—or understood—the source material.

The success of the film all starts with the screenwriters. D.V. DeVincentis, John Cusack, and Steve Pink read the book and right away saw themselves in the story. While Hornby's presence is felt consistently when you watch the film, the screenwriters were never shy about bringing their own interpretation into the mix. They understood who these characters were, what type of story Nick was trying to tell, and also, what type of story they were trying to tell.

It's been nearly thirty years since the book came out and nearly twenty-five years since the movie came out. In that time, the legend of *High Fidelity* has only grown. Any author should consider themselves lucky to get one adaptation out of something they've written. *High Fidelity* has spawned a movie, a 2006 musical, and a 2020 TV series on Hulu. Surely there have to be further retellings in the future.

High Fidelity may feature references to whatever was going on in the culture in that moment, but the reason it is timeless is because it doesn't matter what the references are. You can look past a reference that may feel irrelevant by today's standards. What stands out is the passion behind the person making said reference. We all have a similar passion deep down inside of us.

Now with that all being said, it's time to, once and for all, try to answer that age-old question What came first? The music or the misery?

1

"The Book"

Nick Hornby never worked in a record shop. He wants to make that clear. Despite this, he has gotten many letters from admirers over the years recalling precisely which record shop they remember him working in. Only it was somebody else, not him. He also gets letters from people who can't believe he based the record store in *High Fidelity* on the record store that they work in. He didn't do that, either.

He shrugs off the latter by saying, "I think maybe they're all a bit similar."[1]

Instead, the initial inspiration for Hornby—who was a journalist turned author—to write a book like *High Fidelity* came out of a desire to do something different. Hornby's first book, *Fever Pitch*, came out in 1992. That first book was a memoir that was all about his football obsession. When it was released in 1992, it sold over a million copies in the UK and received nearly universal acclaim. Not bad for a first book, huh?

Fever Pitch even got two film adaptations. First up, in 1997, was a British adaptation starring Colin Firth and Ruth Gemmell with Hornby writing the screenplay and David Evans directing it. Then in 2005, the film got an American adaptation starring Jimmy Fallon and Drew Barrymore with Bobby and Peter Farrely directing, based on a screenplay written by Lowell Ganz and Babaloo Mandel. This version turned football—which would have been called soccer in America anyway—into baseball.

When a writer finds a formula that works, there tends to be a certain kneejerk reaction from the industry essentially saying *This is great. This is what Nick Hornby does.* After just how successful *Fever Pitch* was, particularly after the book was released in paperback, there was a certain expectation for Hornby to tackle another memoir, maybe even something else in the world of sports? After all, it worked the first time. Why couldn't it work again?

But as far as Hornby was concerned, he didn't have another memoir in him at that point. While he has said in interviews that *Fever Pitch* was the "easiest thing to write" due to it being a memoir, he also went on to admit that if he tried to write something like that later on in his career, it'd be "older, wiser, and more boring, because one of the things that made the book was the lack of perspective."[2]

Needless to say, Hornby wasn't interested in repeating himself.

This time around, he wanted to write his first novel. He had an idea to write about a romantic relationship through the male prism. There had, of course, been lots of books about romance and relationships through the female prism, which was something Hornby was quite fond of. But there hadn't been a lot that had been done during that time period from the guy's perspective.

Additionally, the notion of opening the book with an ending—as we see Rob and Laura's relationship in shambles—and ending the book with a beginning—which stood for their new beginning together—intrigued Hornby. So he went back to the same publisher he had worked with on *Fever Pitch*, Gollancz, with the idea for his first novel.

Initially, his publishers were not too keen on the idea of Hornby doing something different. They kept on pitching him ideas for ghost writing biographies of football managers, which would've been a particularly easy trap for a new author to fall into. Instead, he stuck to his guns and insisted on the idea he had for his next book. Luckily for Hornby, the paperback edition of *Fever Pitch* had just come out and was performing exceptionally well.

With that in mind, the publisher relented and greenlit *High Fidelity*.

Setting this story in a record store with the lead character being a music obsessive was basically an afterthought. Hornby already knew the direction he wanted to take the central story in. He knew all the beats that he wanted to hit. The core foundation of *High Fidelity* was born simply out of Hornby asking himself *Alright, so what will this guy do for work?*

"I thought one of the only things I knew anything about or could write about with any great enthusiasm was a job in a record store," Hornby says, "just because I had spent all my life in them."[3]

Once it was settled that Rob would own a record store, everything else started falling into place. While the key component to *High Fidelity* is the love story at the center, setting the story in the world of music just seemed like the perfect fit for a guy like Rob.

Again, Hornby's time spent in record shops was merely as a fan of music. He did, however, have friends who worked in record shops. The record store that he had in his imagination when he wrote the book was actually fairly small, just as most record shops are. While he didn't base the record store on any one store, there was a specific store he frequented that he thought about while writing. It was a record store located next to the Camden Town underground station, called Rock On.

This was a store so small that you couldn't have two people browsing back-to-back in there. This was exactly the sort of aesthetic he wanted to create for the book. The store, which Hornby named Championship Vinyl, couldn't be anywhere that was glamorous or large in scale. It had to be the type of place that Rob couldn't wait to get the hell out of. It had to feel like a weight that was holding him back from moving on to whatever it was he wanted to do next with his life.

Of course, Hornby did have to take the record store out of Camden Town and relocate it to some place more remote where people wouldn't feel as inclined to go. When you read the book, that shift works. Because it's not in an especially populated area, the stage is now set that the record shop isn't doing particularly well, which only adds to Rob's overall frustration. You get the sense that the store is barely hanging on by a thread most days.

Despite the fact that the record store isn't especially thriving, the book doesn't spend too much time focusing on that. It's not about the fact that fewer and fewer people were buying vinyl in the mid-1990s. With the exception of the occasional passing mention, the book's not a commentary on how media was changing. Instead, the focus is on the love of music as a whole and the music tastes of those that were actually in the shop as opposed to harping about those who weren't there.

As for Hornby's personal love of music, that was born out of the *New Music Express*. A staple for any British music obsessive, the *New Music Express*—which is also known as NME—started as a newspaper in 1952. However, the publication got its start even before then as the *Accordion Times and Musical Express*. The *Accordion Times and Musical Express* was purchased by Maurice Kinn, a local music producer. He rebranded it as *New Music Express*, and thus a legend was born.

By the 1970s, it was a standard in the UK. If you wanted to know the ins and the outs of the music culture, discover what people were listening to, and to learn about bands you'd never heard of, you turned to NME. It was during the 1970s that Nick Hornby first discovered *New Music Express*. To this day, he describes NME as being an important part of his culture, and he recalls waiting for it to come out every Thursday.

The writing was really good and really funny. There was definitely a very defined aesthetic taste in NME. And I used to find that quite a lot about books and movies through not only the journalists, but people were encouraged to talk about that stuff in interviews. And I think it was quite different at that time, NME.[4]

It would stand to reason that the characters in *High Fidelity* would also read *New Music Express*. That's because Hornby saw Rob as being an extension of himself in certain ways.

I was dramatizing my own sense of purposelessness and drifting over the previous 10 years or so. That feeling of maybe being edged out of the mainstream of life. Partly by not knowing what you wanted to do. Partly because your interests are so uncommercial in lots of ways. Passion for rock and roll and no musical talent doesn't necessarily give you the most straightforward life. And I identified with that character in all sorts of ways.[5]

All of that being said, Hornby also had enough perspective on the character to put some distance between the two of them. Rob was constructed to be a lot less reasonable than Hornby was and also way more lost in his own disappointment.

Within Rob, there were also blended elements of people Hornby knew. These elements are not so direct that those who influenced the character would be able to notice it. The more that Hornby developed and shaped Rob, the more Rob had a life of his own. Those who helped inspire the character were instead present in spirit more than anything literal on the page.

A recurring theme in the book is an ongoing fascination with categorizing all of the pop culture Rob and his friends surround themselves with into lists. All of these lists are relegated to being the top five, and this is present throughout the book.

Hornby recalls a conversation he had with a friend once that served as the genesis for the top five lists. His friend had expressed his wish to see a publication that was nothing but top five lists, stripping away any ranking explanations or journalistic opinions beyond the list itself.

Hornby thought this was an interesting idea, and when it came time to write the book, he included the top five idea in there. This was long before the idea of lists or ranks made its way into the public consciousness even further via the Internet. There were no clickbait or Buzzfeed-type lists when Hornby was working on the book. Now, of course, those lists are far more prominent on the Internet than the journalism that his friend was trying to avoid in the first place.

"They are my friend's idea, really," says Hornby in retrospect. "You can look at Metacritic and see every record ranked from the last three months. What's got great reviews, what's got mediocre reviews. You don't have to read any of that other stuff."[6]

Another thing that Hornby took to doing with the book was to use his time as a school teacher in a rather unique way. Before becoming a journalist and eventually an author, Hornby taught English in the 1980s. One thing he always kept was a roster of the names of all of the kids he'd taught.

If he was working on a book and couldn't quite think of a good surname for a specific character, he'd open up his old roster and select the name of one of his former students at random. Given how name-heavy a book like *High Fidelity* is when Rob is listing his ex-girlfriends and people he encounters by their full name, this tool came in handy. Some of those students even wound up in the final product.

For instance, Rob's first girlfriend is Alison Ashworth. Alison was also the name of Nick Hornby's first girlfriend. Ashworth was the first person on his school's roll call.

Another thing Hornby was insistent on when writing the book was not to have any sports references in *High Fidelity*. Having sports references would've been too widely expected after *Fever Pitch*. As you quickly gather about Hornby, he will go out of his way to avoid all expectations.

Still, he did allow himself one small sports-related Easter egg that he hid in the book. Another one of Rob's girlfriends is named Charlie Nicholson. In the 1980s, there was an Arsenal football player by the name of Charlie Nichols.

Hornby's insistence on steering clear of what was to be expected paid off. He created this entirely new world, complete with characters that—at one time or another—we all know in our own lives. Everybody knows a guy like Rob, who remains so keyed in to his own world and his own problems, that it seems like he doesn't have much room in his life for anyone else. Everyone knows music snobs like Barry or Dick, who know that they know more about music than you do and are not afraid to rub your face in it.

When *High Fidelity* was released in 1995, the response to the book was overwhelmingly positive pretty immediately.

Suzanne Moore of the *Guardian* wrote, "Reading *High Fidelity* is like listening to a great single. You know it's wonderful from the minute it goes on, and as soon as it's over, you want to hear it again because it makes you feel young, and grown-up, and puts a stupid grin on your face all at the same time. If this book was a record, we would be calling it an instant classic."[7]

Joseph Olshan for *Entertainment Weekly* wrote, "Nick Hornby, a well-known and respected London journalist, has written a candid and comic first novel that bumps along like a diamond needle over the flawed vinyl album of Rob's life."[8]

Mark Jolly for the *New York Times* observed that "plain and simple language—Mr. Hornby's trademark—is supposed to wrestle the truth from all literary artifice. But as with pop music itself, beneath the simplicity lies a multitude of nuances."[9]

In the UK and Europe, *High Fidelity* did quite well. Coming from the author of *Fever Pitch*, the book garnered a lot of attention, received critical praise, and quickly became a bestseller. In the United States, however, it was a bit of a different story.

When *Fever Pitch* was released in the United States, Hornby notes that "nobody noticed it." Despite getting good reviews, he was essentially a first-time author in the United States, so the book sales reflected as much. Then, as the paperback edition came out, the tide started to change.

"I did a book tour then," says Hornby, "and there were plenty of people who came out to see me on the coasts—it was a struggle in the rest of the U.S. I did an interview for Fresh Air with Terry Gross, and just about everyone who came to hear me read had heard me on NPR. I was very grateful to her for her support."[10]

Responses this good would be enough to draw the attention of Hollywood, surely. Well, they would've been if the book hadn't already been optioned before it was released in the United States.

2

The Fast Option

When an author writes a book, most times that is the end goal. You've got a story that you need to tell, and you can only hope that people will like it. The idea of movie rights or any sort of afterlife beyond the page is all an afterthought. And for Hornby, it was no different.

Also, it wasn't as if *High Fidelity* was calling out to be adapted into the film world. After all, there're so many obstacles that you'd face when trying to adapt this into a film. What could you possibly do with source material that features as much internal narration as *High Fidelity* does?

"Well, this is a book that is set inside a guy's head, inside a record store," Hornby said in an interview. "It doesn't really define cinematic."[1]

Hornby added, "The narrative climax of this book is somebody makes somebody else a tape. That's it. It really wasn't written with one eye on the film rights."

High Fidelity was released in the United States on September 16, 1995. Yet over three months before the book ever hit shelves in the United States, a deal was made for the film rights. This was hardly the first time something like that had happened nor would it be the last. Most famously, the producers of *Jaws* secured the film rights before the book even hit the publication stage. Still, it is a rarity and nothing short of a crowning achievement for an author whenever it does happen.

On June 9, 1995, British film magazine *Screen International* published an article stating that the film rights had been optioned for Hornby's forthcoming book. Already, there was a lot of attention on the novel given the success of Hornby's *Fever Pitch* in the UK. So the fact that the option happened as quickly as it did should come as little surprise.

For Hornby, however, it certainly was a surprise and not something he was anticipating. Nevertheless, Touchstone wound up purchasing the rights for $500,000 with Mike Newell attached to direct.[2]

By the mid-1990s, Mike Newell was a sought-after director. Newell started working in 1964 as a director for television shows in Britain. Some of his earliest directorial work included episodes of *Coronation Street*; *The Fellows*; *Spindoe*; *Her Majesty's Pleasure*; and countless other shows in the 1960s and 1970s. He eventually made his theatrical film directorial debut with *The Awakening*, which starred Charlton Heston.

From there, he built up a solid reputation for himself as a director of films such as *Bad Blood*; *Dance with a Stranger*; *The Good Father*; *Amazing Grace and Chuck*; *Soursweet*; *Enchanted April*; *Into the West*; and the smash hit *Four Weddings and a Funeral*. The latter had just been released in May the year before, and made over $245 million at the box office against a $4.4 million budget. Newell received the coveted BAFTA Award for Best Direction for the film. So naturally, having him sign onto *High Fidelity* was nothing short of a huge score.

Mike Newell got involved with the project through a woman named Betsy Beers, who was working for him at the time. According to Newell, her job was to search for potential material for him to direct. Just as she had with *Donnie Brasco*, which Newell directed and was released in 1997, she learned about this new book called

High Fidelity. Newell wound up getting his hands on a copy, liked it very much, and promptly signed on to direct the film adaptation.

When Hornby's first book *Fever Pitch* was turned into a movie in 1997, Hornby had written the screenplay. This served as the only time in his career that he adapted his own source material. With *High Fidelity*, he had no interest in doing the same.

"I came to the decision, which I've stuck to pretty much ever since," says Hornby, "which is *I just spent two years writing this. Fever Pitch* had taken five years to become a British movie and I had been involved in the script of that. I always thought, *I'd really rather get on with something else.*"[3]

On top of that, Hornby's career as an author started when he was thirty-five, after having worked for years as a journalist. So with that came a feeling of needing to make up for lost time. He wanted to just keep moving on to the next thing and telling the next story. Why say something he'd already said before?

Instead, the job of penning the script went to a young American screenwriter named Scott Rosenberg. A graduate of UCLA, Rosenberg's first feature film for Miramax, *Things to Do in Denver When You're Dead*. While the film didn't necessarily light the world on fire, it did boast an impressive cast that included Andy Garcia, Christopher Lloyd, William Forsythe, Jack Warden, Treat Williams, Steve Buscemi, and Christopher Walken. And as Miramax and Touchstone both fell under the Disney umbrella, it makes sense that they chose to bring Rosenberg onto the film.

When Rosenberg was first approached about writing the script, however, he was hesitant. This was mainly due to the fact that he already owed six scripts and naturally wasn't looking to take on a seventh. However, he wound up reading the book anyway. He was hooked right away. As he was a huge music lover and a self-described "tremendous commitment phobe," the material wound up resonating with him instantly. He saw himself in the character of Rob so much so that he actually wondered *Who is this Nick Hornby guy and how has he been living in my brain?*[4]

Despite his other commitments, Rosenberg signed on to write the script. Rosenberg's initial pitch to move the story across the Atlantic and set it in Boston was received well by Newell. Rosenberg, who is from Boston, says he knew he had to set the film in a second city as opposed to setting it in Los Angeles or New York. He also felt that Boston was not unlike London in as much as they are both a bit of a melting pot of cultures.

With a direction fully formed, Rosenberg got to work on the script.

One of the first things that became clear to Rosenberg while he was working on the film was that Rob could not be played by the leading men of the moment. At that time, the leading men in Hollywood were people like George Clooney, Johnny Depp, Brad Pitt, and Matt Damon. According to Rosenberg, Rob had to be someone who could walk into a bar and wouldn't immediately have women fawning all over him.

The person Rosenberg was pushing to play Rob was Jim Carrey. This was before Jim Carrey had shown off his dramatic chops with *The Truman Show*. At that point, Carrey was known for *In Living Color* and his subsequent breakout film roles that included *Ace Ventura: Pet Detective*; *The Mask*; *Dumb and Dumber*; and *The Cable Guy*. These characters had a tendency to be more broad and over the top than Rob called for. But still, Rosenberg had a good sense that Carrey could prove that he was far more than the guy who talks out of his ass or mimics "the most annoying sound in the world."

"I opened this movie with a scene in Pompei—back in its volcano day—with this young man about to roll the dice," says Rosenberg, mirroring a scene in the book. "He doesn't want to. He says 'I'm a poet. I'm not a gambler.' His friends talk him into it. And then just as he's about to roll the dice, you hear this boom from the volcano above and the volcano erupts."[5]

Rosenberg's opening scene continues.

> Then, flash forward to where there's Pompei, and it's frozen in ash. And there's this one body and he's holding this dice. And then the archeologist goes, "Oh that guy must have been a gambler." It's Rob's narration; and he says, "You can get stuck. It's very easy to get stuck in a way that was not necessarily how you thought of yourself."

Obviously, a scene like that would have eaten up way too much of the film's budget. That scene alone would have cost a good chunk of the $30 million that the film eventually got made for years later.

In his draft, Rosenberg insists that he stuck as closely to the book as possible. But according to Rosenberg, Newell was very into the idea of gentrification and how the neighborhood the record store is in had changed with the times.

So Rosenberg included the aspect of a competing record store in his draft, something that was not in the source material. He wrote into the script that a large, multimillion dollar corporation was opening up across the street, sort of like a Virgin Megastore. In the 1990s, Virgin Megastores were the biggest source of competition for the mom-and-pop record stores. So a similar type of store was added to the film's plot.

At this point, Newell got busy with another project and moved on to focus on that project for the time being. Rosenberg says he was then asked if he wanted to continue with the project. However, after two years, Rosenberg felt it was time to move on. He opted to instead work with Wes Craven over at Dimension on a werewolf biker film.

After a very fast option process, *High Fidelity* now found itself with a director or a screenwriter. This is a classic Hollywood story.

Just because all the stars are seemingly aligning for your film to get made doesn't mean anything. It can all end just as quickly as it started. As Hornby recalls, it was at this point that the film "just disappeared for four years."

> I didn't know anything about it. I didn't know where it had gone or what had happened to it. I now understand that this is pretty standard for the process. I've had some things optioned, and they've all disappeared in the same way. But at the time, I did not have that experience, so I just presumed it was just dead.[6]

It would take some time, but the project was indeed resurrected thanks to Kathy Nelson, who was working for Joe Roth, who served as the chairman of Disney from 1994 until 2000. Nelson first connected with Roth while she was senior vice president at MCA Records for its MCA Soundtracks. Nelson came with a successful track record while at MCA, working on films like *Pulp Fiction*; *Beverly Hills Cop* and its sequel *The Commitments*; and *Miami Vice*.

By 1995, the name Kathy Nelson had been generating its own buzz when she was working on the soundtrack for the film *Dangerous Minds*. Nelson picked the song "Gangsta's Paradise" by Coolio to open the film. The film itself was critically panned, which did little to improve its success at the box office. But "Gangsta's Paradise" was praised and even won an MTV Music Video Award that year for Best Rap Song.

Roth had heard about this and wanted to meet the person whom he felt had saved *Dangerous Minds*. After meeting with Nelson, he offered her the coveted position of president of music for all of Disney.

According to Nelson, one day while at Disney she got a call from an old friend from her MCA days named Roger Ames, who was then president of London Records. "Oh, while you're at Disney," Ames told Nelson, "they own a property of a book that is just amazing called *High Fidelity*." Nelson then inquired with Joe Roth to find out whether or not Disney had it. It turns out Disney did still have it, and it was about to expire.[7]

Joe Roth loved the material and was a huge champion of getting it made. Before his position at Disney, Roth himself had directed a few films in the 1980s including *Streets of Gold*; *Revenge of the Nerds II: Nerds in Paradise*; and *Coupe de Ville*. He later said in an interview that if he wasn't running the studio at the time, he would have wanted to direct it himself.[8]

Now that there was interest in the film again, the studio had to find someone to write the script. Kathy Nelson immediately thought of an old friend she'd just worked with on 1997's *Grosse Pointe Blank*, John Cusack.

According to Cusack,

> I had made *Grosse Point Blank* with Joe Roth and Kathy Nelson over at Touchstone. And we had sort of just finished a film where music was super important. We got Joe Stummer, we managed to get David Bowie and Queen's "Under Pressure." And so we had gone through the process of making a cool soundtrack and Joe and Kathy knew how important music was to me, to the movies that I was producing.[9]

Nelson recalls,

> I sent Johnny the book and I said, "You've got to read this book." And he called me back and said, "Oh my God. I loved it. Just think, it would give us an excuse to listen to music for hours." And I said, "I know. You are this guy." And that was really the birth of the movie *High Fidelity*.[10]

By this point, John Cusack was already a big draw as an actor. Cusack's first role on camera was in 1983's *Class*, which starred Jacqueline Bisset and two of Cusack's fellow 1980s teenage heartthrob staples, Rob Lowe and Andrew McCarthy.

During this period in the 1980s, more and more film production began to take place in Chicago. As a direct result, a more watchful eye was being paid to local talent. Cusack, naturally, was a strong standout, demonstrating not just impressive acting chops but a natural charm that would serve him well in all of the parts he played.

After *Class*, he had supporting roles in *Sixteen Candles* and *Grandville, USA*. By 1985, Cusack had his first shot at a starring role in *The Sure Thing*. With Cusack being sixteen at the time, the film's director, Rob Reiner, reportedly wrote off Cusack as being too young for the part. However, once Cusack auditioned, Reiner came around and realized he was perfect for the role. The film was met with a positive reaction, with a lot of praise going to Cusack, citing it as a breakout role for the young Evanston native.

Cusack followed up the success of *The Sure Thing* with a slew of films including *Better Off Dead . . .* ; *Stand By Me*; *One Crazy Summer*; *Hot Pursuit*; *Tapeheads*; *Eight Men Out*; and a film that he is perhaps best known for, Cameron Crowe's *Say Anything*.

Say Anything solidified John Cusack as a romantic leading man by this point. As much as *The Sure Thing* could be cited as his breakout role, *Say Anything* can be argued as being the film that helped make him a legitimate movie star. After his turn as Lloyd Dobler in the film opposite Ione Skye, you were hard-pressed to find a woman or teenage girl who didn't immediately fall in love with John Cusack.

As a result, it would've been so easy for Cusack to keep riding that wave of being the romantic lead. Much like what Nick Hornby encountered after *Fever Pitch,* once you've proven you're good at something in Hollywood, those are the types of offers you get. Of course, once you start taking those offers, you come to realize that you've been placed in this box and suddenly you only get to be *that* guy. It's a slippery slope that actors generally don't think much about until they're in that position.

Post–*Say Anything*, Cusack was looking to branch out. His next film was a departure from the traditional romantic lead type. In *The Grifters*, Cusack played a small-time grifter, a role that was a clear departure from Dobler.

The film was a crime thriller that paired him up with director Stephen Frears. Frears himself was fresh off the commercial success of *Dangerous Liaisons*. *The Grifters* actually originated with Martin Scorsese, who eventually brought the film to Frears to direct. After Frears came on board, Scorsese stepped into the role of producer.

Thankfully, the shift wound up working out for Cusack. The film was critically praised and even nabbed four Academy Award nominations, including Best Director for Frears and Best Adapted Screenplay for Donald E. Westlake.

Following the success of *The Grifters*, Cusack starred in *True Colors*; *Money for Nothing*; *Bullets Over Broadway*; *The Road to Wellville*; and *Con Air*. Cusack had successfully branched out by this point, and was taking on roles that—with perhaps the exception of *Con Air*, which was Cusack's first foray into the blockbuster world—served as a vehicle for his abilities as an actor. This was something that probably wouldn't have had the same impact if he kept playing the Dobler type.

Regardless of the types of roles he was taking on, one thing was certain. Cusack's natural charm always managed to shine right through. He possessed this rare gift to make any character likable. This extends to characters that were purposefully written to be unlikable. With that in mind, that is what makes him the ideal choice to play a character like Rob in *High Fidelity*.

Rob is complicated as a character. Not only are his flaws clearly visible to the audience, they are just as visible to himself. He hides nothing, and perhaps that's why we identify with him. He exudes this brutal honesty that somehow makes his being a self-described asshole more tolerable.

Given the nature of Rob's character, it was important to make sure the person who played him was likable enough that you didn't grow sick of the character halfway through the film. Regardless of his choices, you still need to be able to root for Rob at the end of the film. You want him to get something of a win. Miscasting could have easily made audiences walk away with more of a disdain for Rob.

But someone like John Cusack was able to bring even more depth to the character and fully flesh him out. To put it frankly, there was nobody else who was a better fit for *High Fidelity* than John Cusack.

It was *Grosse Pointe Blank* in 1997, however, that showcased another side of Cusack. It was his first credit as a screenwriter. Cusack was a cowriter on the film alongside high school friends D.V. DeVincentis and Steve Pink. The film follows a hitman who returns to his old school to attend his high school reunion.

The film as a whole received favorable reviews from critics and also doubled its money. It was an action comedy that seemed to have a pretty dark yet consistently comedic edge to it. The script seemed to garner universal praise, which as first-time screenwriters, is all they could really ask for.

So it would make total sense that upon completion, Nelson, Roth, and the rest of the gang at Disney would have Cusack, Pink, and DeVincentis in mind to helm the story of *High Fidelity*.

DeVincentis recalls,

> When it came out, everybody kept telling me, "You've got to read this book. It's you. You have to read this book." So I read the book and I loved it. I related to it so much. I happened to have always been a music obsessive. I've got hundreds of records. I get into these types of conversations all the time. And it was

sort of written by somebody who understood this and was also poking fun at it in the perfect way.[11]

When he first read the book, however, DeVincentis felt his "pleasure reading was being intercepted by my business brain."[12]

So while reading it, he fended off any voice in the back of his head that was suggesting that maybe this book could be something he could adapt. DeVincentis didn't want his enjoyment of reading the book to be diminished by his self-described business brain. It wasn't until a few years later when he received a similar call from Kathy Nelson that he agreed to do so.

Says Pink,

> The book is brilliant because it's universal. It touches on universal themes like love and relationships and dysfunction and ridiculousness and a nerd level passion for something, and in this case being music. We identified with that. We were all music nerds who thought we were the coolest people ever, while at the same time, being totally dysfunctional and ridiculous people growing up.[13]

But the creative relationship between John Cusack, D.V. DeVincentis, and Steve Pink didn't begin with *Grosse Point Blank*. It actually went all the way back to their high school days in the 1980s.

Cusack, DeVincentis, and Pink all attended Evanston Township High School together. Cusack and Pink were a year ahead of DeVincentis. DeVincentis first became aware of Cusack when he was a freshman in high school, and they started hanging out soon after. During that time, the two of them shared a bond in their love of music and absurd comedy.

One of DeVincentis's earliest memories of their friendship was when they were hanging out at Cusack's house at three in the morning one night and Cusack decided to call in to a sports radio show. Ever the passionate baseball fan, with the Chicago Cubs being his team of choice, the fifteen-year-old Cusack was able to hold his own with the hosts. Then, he took them on a wild ride.

"He's on with these guys, and he's having a regular conversation with them," recalls DeVincentis.

> And then John says something weird. And then there's the slightest pause, but they roll with it because they're making good radio. And then John says something a little weirder, and takes them down a road in a different direction. And they kind of follow because it's going well. And then he gets them in a weirder place and a weirder place and a weirder place. And I'm losing my mind. Watching him toy with these guys and this was an absurd exploration of what he was talking about improvisationally.[14]

At their high school, there was an annual talent show called YAMO. YAMO has long been a staple of Evanston Township High School and it is still performed to this day. Up until that point, Steve Pink had not been particularly close to John Cusack or D.V. DeVincentis. That all changed their senior year thanks to YAMO.

"I was chosen to be one of the writers of the show along with Cusack," Pink remembers. "We had acted in little sketches over the years, but we weren't really friends through high school. People are like, 'Oh, you were high school buddies.' Well, we became really close our senior year."[15]

Pink mainly served as the writer and director of YAMO that year but he also wound up acting in one of the sketches alongside D.V. DeVincentis. The two of them wound up becoming close their senior year. From that point forward, Cusack, DeVincentis, and Pink had their own little tight-knit crew going on.

"Kind of around the same time, John started to become famous," says DeVincentis. "Which was wild. It was definitely surreal. It became an experience for all of us. It became the beginning of a long period in my life, which continues to this day, where I experience so many things as a result of being close with John and being colleagues with John and friends with John."[16]

Acting was a family affair for the Cusack family. Cusack's father, Dick, had been an advertising executive for years before changing careers in 1970. By 1971, he had won an Emmy Award for the documentary *The Committee*, which was about abortion. Then in the early 1980s, he started getting small roles acting in films starting with *My Bodyguard* before following it up with *Class*, which costarred both John and his sister Joan.

Joan Cusack's first role was alongside her father in *My Bodyguard*. Aside from also appearing in *Class* alongside with John, she worked with him in *Sixteen Candles*; *Grandview, U.S.A.*; *Broadcast News*; *Say Anything*; *Grosse Pointe Blank*; *Cradle Will Rock*; *War, Inc.*; and eventually *High Fidelity*.

Aside from the films alongside her brother, Joan Cusack also has a long and solid resume in Hollywood, including racking up two Academy Award nominations from her work in the films *Working Girl* and *In and Out*.

After graduation, Cusack went to NYU, but dropped out after a year. Pink went off to Berkeley, and DeVincentis went off to film school. Despite going their separate ways, they all stayed connected during that period.

In the late 1980s, Cusack, DeVincentis, and Pink founded a theater company in Chicago named New Crime Productions, which would later become their film production company name as well. Pink describes the company as being a rival of the well-known Lookinglass Theater company.

One of the many theater productions they did was a stage adaptation of Hunter S. Thompson's *Fear and Loathing in Las Vegas* in 1991. This was, of course, after Cusack had already made a big name for himself in Hollywood and was one of the most promising young stars of Gen X. Cusack and Pink both directed the show, which starred Cusack's brother Billy and fellow Evanston Township High School pal Jeremy Piven.

Piven and Cusack actually went back even farther than that. Their parents—Byrne and Joyce Piven and Dick and Ann Cusack respectively—were close friends, meaning that Cusack and Piven had known each other before they could even walk. Of course, the two of them would wind up working together on various projects over the years, movies like *One Crazy Summer*; *Say Anything*; *The Grifters*; *The Player*; *Bob Roberts*; *Grosse Point Blank*; *Serendipity*; and *Runaway Jury*. The only person whom Cusack worked with more during his career was his sister Joan.

Fear and Loathing in Las Vegas ran for six months in Chicago. After its run, Pink and DeVincentis both wound up in Hollywood and worked on a screenplay adaptation of *Fear and Loathing in Las Vegas*.

In the early 1990s, Cusack and Pink had a deal at Paramount. One day, Laila Nabulsi—the producer who had the film rights for *Fear and Loathing in Las Vegas* and was attempting to get the adaptation going—called their office on the Paramount lot. She was asking their opinion on whom she should get to pen the script for the film. Pink and DeVincentis threw their hats into the ring.

Her immediate response was "No, you guys. I want a real screenwriter."

Undeterred, the boys decided to call up Hunter S. Thompson and asked him for his blessing to go off and write the script. Once that was granted, Laila agreed to read what they wrote but wasn't going to commit to making the film.

Over the course of the next two weeks, they cranked out a screenplay. They were clearly on a mission, knowing full well that the prospects of ever getting the job were already so far out of reach that they had to act as fast as possible. With nothing to lose and loads of passion and determination on their side, they delivered a script that was well liked by everyone. Despite this, according to DeVincentis, Laila stood firm on wanting to get a proven screenwriter.

"I bare her no ill will about that at all," DeVincentis says. "I get it. She wanted a journeyman. This was her shot at this property that everyone knows around the world. She didn't want to do it with a couple of first timers. Especially since she had never produced a movie. So it makes total sense."[17]

Pink, however, recalls that they were actually closer to getting the movie made. According to Pink, they wrote the script as a vehicle for Cusack. Alex Cox, the director of *Sid and Nancy*, even came on board to direct the film.

"Alex Cox somehow got us fired and then John fired," recalls Pink. "And then he went and got Johnny Depp and then they were going to go off and do the movie together. But then Johnny Depp fired Alex Cox and got Terry Gilliam."[18]

At one point, their work on *Fear and Loathing in Las Vegas* got DeVincentis and Pink a job at Paramount writing a proof-of-concept short film for RuPaul. While this never went anywhere either, for DeVincentis it was his first time actually getting paid to work on a writing project.

Thankfully, the opportunity to work on *Grosse Point Blank* came along not too long after, and Cusack, DeVincentis, and Pink finally had their first film as a screenwriting team under their belt.

Back to *High Fidelity*. After getting the greenlight from Joe Roth, Cusack, DeVincentis, and Pink got to work on the script. However, this being the film business, just being brought on to write a screenplay never guarantees that it will actually come to fruition. There are far more movies that have been in development than those that have ever seen the light of day.

And then it happened. The moment they realized that the movie was officially going to happen.

As Pink recalls,

> One day we were on the Disney lot, for some reason and Joe Roth, who is getting out of the parking lot, pulls over. He pauses and says, "Hey, how's it going on the script? Because I'm making that movie." Then he drove off, and we're like "Holy shit. We better get to work. The chairman of the studio just paused to tell us he's making the movie."[19]

With that, they were off to the races.

3

Finding Frears

When you're helming any kind of production for film or TV, there are many different opportunities for things to go wrong at any point in the process. It's very easy to hire the wrong screenwriter, the wrong director, or cast the wrong leads.

There's also the danger of having too many cooks in the kitchen. This is a problem that you'll see when everyone is trying to bring their own special ingredients to the recipe. By the time it's ready to go, it's uneven—and even inedible.

So what's the secret to having a successful production? There's not one specific thing you can point to. Every project is its own unique beast with its own set of advantages and disadvantages. That being said, if the script is written from a place that reads as tonally sincere and coming from a place of passion for the material, that much is apparent to the reader.

In the case of *High Fidelity*, Cusack, DeVincentis, and Pink could relate to the overarching elements of the story. As the three of them were all music obsessives in their own right, they understood just how sacred Rob, Dick, and Barry held that record shop and all the musical goodness that laid within the walls.

Then there's also the relationship factor of the story, which to this day remains as universal as ever. Even as the dating scene has changed since the book came out in 1995, the trials and tribulations of relationships remain unchanged.

Any person who has ever been in a relationship from here until the end of time has the same internal thoughts that Rob has at one point or another. It's whether or not they express those thoughts in the same way Rob does in the story that's up for debate. You may not be speaking them out loud, but all of us—both men and women—have shared those sentiments at one time or another.

So much of what was in the book managed to make the leap over to the screenplay. One liberty that Cusack, DeVincentis, and Pink knew that they had to take was the location. They felt that to best tell the version of the story that they were looking to tell, the story would have to jump across the pond and land right in their native Chicago.

Naturally at the time that this was first announced, it was more-or-less written off by fans of the book. A typical response from many fans was that they felt it was yet another example of an American bastardization. This is the fear that Hollywood will take something good from another culture and appropriate it, not because this fits the narrative of the story they're looking to tell, but simply because they want to use American actors instead of British actors.

But to the screenwriters, it wasn't about just moving the material to Chicago because they could. This is how they'd best be able to bring the most authentic version of the source material to the screen. For example, had they tried to set it in London, it would be their interpretation of what it'd be like to be a music obsessive in London. But by setting it in their native Chicago, there was no escaping the amount of realism they could bring to the project.

Plus when you really sit down and take a closer look, you'll notice just how many striking similarities there are between Chicago and London.

Says Pink,

> I feel like we came from blue collar families, or middle-class families-ish, lower-middle-class families. It's a post-industrial

town that has a vibrant counter culture. Chicago has always had that, like London. We all identified with that, because there's almost no limit of all the cultural stuff you could get into in Chicago in terms of the music scene and the theater scene.[1]

For DeVincentis,

It dovetails right into all of my record stores. It dovetails right into my friends' bars and my friends' bands and the conversations that I've had throughout my whole life, teen into adult life in Chicago. Like, this is easy for me. I could transpose this thing to it effortlessly.[2]

For his part, Cusack was able to see beneath the layers of the music. To him, that was the sole difference between Hornby's Rob, Dick, and Barry and John, D.V., and Steve. They had all grown up—as had so many others in their generation—with a deep love and appreciation of British rock. In the book, Cusack recalls that their music tastes were entirely soul, rhythm, and blues.

"Once you switched that," Cusack said, "it was the same guys. It was just a male confessional, and also about a love affair with music and themes about how music is autobiographical in our lives."[3]

While the decision to flip the script was met with outrage from incensed book and music lovers who, let's be honest, would be watching the film regardless, the one man whose opinion should matter the most on the swap saw absolutely no issue with it. To Nick Hornby, it was such a nonissue.

That seemed to me a ridiculous thing to have any objection to. I had just started going on tour with the book, and whether I went to New York or whether I went to Hamburg, no one ever said to me, "Oh, that's what it's like to be English." They always said, "Well I'm like this and my brother's like this and my boyfriend's like this." And the nationality of Rob really had no bearing on anything.[4]

"He realized that the book had translated into a bunch of languages and he got letters from all over the world saying how much this book spoke to him," adds DeVincentis. "And he realized that it's about these characters and situations and it's not about a country or a city."[5]

The thing that really impressed Hornby was just how much of a love letter the trio made it to Chicago. It was all very specific to not just the city itself, but the music culture that was so deeply embedded in the city, particularly in Wicker Park.

Another thing that was very important to DeVincentis, Pink, and Cusack was not only setting the film in Chicago but placing the characters in specific neighborhoods that they could actually picture them living in.

"We liked the idea that Rob lived in Roger's Park," says Pink.

> Basically, he didn't live in the cool area of Wicker Park. It's a subtlety, but it was important. Rob isn't cool in that way. Rob lives in Roger's Park. He's a dude who found an apartment he could afford in a quiet neighborhood in Roger's Park. Which is different than the Wicker Park vibe, but that's where his record store is. That's where Double Door is.[6]

These same general rules of writing to specific neighborhoods for each character applied to others in the film as well.

For instance, Charlie's apartment in the script is described as being a "fabulous sophomore design student's studio apartment: White wood floor, white walls, overvarnished door, Doisneaux print on the wall, futon on the floor."[7]

In this case, they envisioned Charlie living closer to the Wicker Park area in a lofty space that was yet-to-be-gentrified.

Even from their very first draft, it was incredibly important to everyone involved that they remain faithful to Hornby's book. This is something that makes *High Fidelity* as a film unique.

"The writing of the movie all came out of conversations that would lead to these kind of ideas that then we would write," Pink says of the writing dynamic between the three of them. "Which is just the natural course of writing, but that's what'd make it so fun. We'd have these really funny discussions about what would be the dynamic between these characters in any given moment. Some of them were similar to our own."[8]

Essentially, how the writing dynamic would break down between the three of them was that DeVincentis and Pink would draft together, Cusack would come in and revise, then the three of them would all draft together. As you can imagine, when you've got three creatives working on a project that each writer holds so dear to themselves, there's no shortage of passionate discussions—and of course debates. Every idea was fair game, meaning that all three of them would make strong arguments about why their idea was the right way to go.

"The top five things I miss about Laura was a really good idea that John had," says DeVincentis. "It was a necessary way to show Rob's real and true love and appreciation for Laura on a deep level that he identified it would need. He went off and wrote that whole scene himself and it was wonderful. It was really, really good for the movie."[9]

In earlier drafts of the script, Rob has even more top five lists that didn't wind up in the final film. Some of Rob's additional top five lists included the following.

Top Five Books

1. *Cash* by Johnny Cash
2. *Snow Crash* by Neil Stevenson

3. *Zen and the Art of Motorcycle Maintenance*
4. *The Trouser Press Guides to Rock*
5. And something by Kurt Vonnegut[10]

Top Five American Films

1. *Blade Runner*
2. *Cool Hand Luke*
3. *The first two* Godfathers, *which we'll count as one*
4. *Taxi Driver*
5. *The Shining*[11]

As a whole, the script remained very loyal to the source material. After all, Nick Hornby had already struck gold with the book. That is why so much of Rob's internal makes its way into the script. How could you possibly improve on Hornby's meticulously detailed writing?

"We tried to be faithful to the book at all times," says Pink. "First principles were *What does the book say and do? What is the beat? What's the moment? What's the story he's expressing? What's the idea? What's this character relationship doing?*"[12]

One thing that did differ from the book, however, was Rob's last name. In the book, he is Rob Fleming. In the film? He is Rob Gordon.

When he first read the script, Nick Hornby assumed that the switch was inspired by the writer Rob Gordon, who wrote the 1995 book *It Came From Memphis*, which details the history of the Memphis alternative music scene.

In actuality, it was not as deep a reference as Hornby assumed it to be. While writing the script, DeVincentis was struggling to remember Rob's last name in the book. He flipped through the book in an attempt to locate it, to no avail. So he just changed Rob's last name to Gordon, which was the surname of a neighborhood family from his childhood.

"I'll tell you, I thought *This is the right man for me*," Hornby admits with a laugh. "I would've done exactly the same."[13]

When it comes to scripts, some screenwriters are more sparing with details than others. Some scripts are more dialogue heavy than detail-oriented. *High Fidelity*, on paper, is a blend of both of those sensibilities. The dialogue—heavily influenced by and expanded on the world Nick Hornby crafted in the novel—is, of course, very well constructed.

That being said, DeVincentis, Pink, and Cusack were just as specific when it came down to every tiny detail in the script. They knew who Rob was, and they knew the world, because Rob's world was their world. They knew his neighborhood, his stereo system, and even his record collection.

Rob's system, they write, is "not a minisystem, not a matching set, but coveted audiophile clutter of McIntosh and Nakamichi, each component from a different era, bought piece by piece in various nanoseconds of being flush."

Rob's music collection is "big thin LPs. Fields of them. We move across them, slowly. . . . They seem to come to rest in an end of a few books. . . . But then the CDs start, and go on, faster and faster, forever, then the singles, then the tapes."

By this point, Cusack was just wrapping up his next film *Pushing Tin*, which coincidentally paired him up with Mike Newell. *Pushing Tin* was in postproduction, and as Newell recalls, Cusack was very, very keen on their doing *High Fidelity* together.

Now that the boys knew that they wanted to set the story in their native Chicago, they had to sell the big step across the Atlantic to Newell. DeVincentis outlined the entire pitch on notecards and pinned them to his dining room wall. He then walked Newell through the pitch.

"At the end of which, he said something so charming and sweet, which was 'Does it have to be in Chicago,'" DeVincentis recalls Newell asking.

> I'm like "Why?" "Could it be in London?" I said, "Yes, but if it were to be in London, you might want to consider getting a British actor and British writers. Why do you think it should be in London?" He said, "Well, the only reason I really think it should be in London is because I have a family and they live there. And I think it would be really nice to make the film around my family."[14]

"I had a daughter who was four or five years old," recalls Newell. "I had been away, of course, making three other movies. So that would've been three movies in the U.S. on the trot with a very young family. And it's quite possible that was—not quite a straw, but more a tree trunk—that broke the camel's back."[15]

Now once again, things were put on the backburner. Newell was busy with postproduction on *Pushing Tin*. Eventually, Disney was eager to just get the film made already. So the decision was made to look for a new director.

When it came to a new director for the film, some names were thrown at the boys. Eventually, it was John Cusack who came up with the idea of approaching Stephen Frears, whom he had previously worked with.

Cusack said in an interview,

> I did a film with him when I was twenty-five called *The Grifters*, and that was an intense, cool film. So I had a good understanding of how he worked. I don't know if everybody else did. But how could they? They hadn't done as much work as I had done. But I sort of knew what he was up to and how to deal with it. But it was great. He's a very intense, creative guy.[16]

Newell, who was now on board solely as an executive producer, attended Cambridge with Stephen Frears. They weren't necessarily close, but they definitely knew each other. In fact, Newell had been a big fan of Frears's film *My Beautiful Launderette*. So he gave it his blessing, and the call was made.

Newell recalls,

> Ultimately we went to Steve to find out if Steve was interested. And Steve said, "Indeed I am interested, yes. There's just one condition. That is if I were to make the film, you would guarantee to be 150 miles away from any town, city, location, wherever I was making the film." In other words, he didn't want me in his hair at all.[17]

Newell agreed to these stipulations. He still received an executive producer credit on the film, but his involvement in the final product was limited to just that credit. That was just fine with Newell, who would've felt awkward if he had any sort of power over one of his contemporaries, particularly when that contemporary was someone as talented and as brilliant as Stephen Frears.

With Newell at least 150 miles away from Chicago, it was official. Stephen Frears was in. If you ask Nick Hornby, though, the way that he found out that Frears would be tackling his first novel on the big screen was rather—shall we say—unconventional.

Hornby remembers,

> I used to buy my cigarettes, when I smoked, from the same kiosk outside Arsenal Underground Station every day. And one day, the guy who ran the kiosk gave me a piece of paper, and on the piece of paper it said, "Phone Stephen Frears at this number." Stephen knew someone who knew that he was a neighbor of mine. And he said, "Can you get this to Nick?" And he said,

"Well I think he goes to the kiosk at the end of my street, so I'll give it to the guy there."[18]

"Well, he always tells that story," Frears responds, saying he has no recollection of the cigarette kiosk. "But I had a friend who lived near the kiosk, so I guess that's how it happened."[19]

What Frears does remember is that call coming in from John Cusack asking him to be involved. He was responsive pretty much right away. He'd read the book within three days of its release in 1999, just as he'd read Hornby's other books. However, the thought of turning the book into a movie never really crossed his mind.

By the time Stephen Frears had signed on to do *High Fidelity*, he had already carved out a name for himself as being one of the most acclaimed and accomplished directors of his generation. After spending a few years working as an assistant director on films like *if . . .* and some TV directing work, he made his first film, *Gumshoe*, in 1971.

After *Gumshoe*, he then went back to working in TV. His next feature film was *The Hit*, followed by 1985's critically acclaimed *My Beautiful Laundrette*, which received BAFTA and Academy Award nominations. After *Laundrette*, Frears made *Prick Up Your Ears* and *Sammy and Rosie Get Laid*. His next two films were two of his biggest successes, *Dangerous Liaisons* and *The Grifters*. This was followed by *Hero*; *Mary Reilly*; *The Van*; and finally *The Hi-Lo Country*, which was released in 1998.

So having someone as respected as Stephen Frears coming on board was nothing short of a big win for the production. And as DeVincentis points out, a personal win for himself.

One night when he was fifteen, two of DeVincentis's friends who worked in a video store had rented *The Hit* and *Prick Up Your Ears*. He noticed a similar energy in both movies, despite their having very different plots. He then discovered it was because both had been directed by the same guy. This changed DeVincentis's outlook on film, as it showed him that it didn't just fall out of the sky. Rather, he started becoming more aware of directors and subsequently did a deep dive into the work of Stephen Frears.

With this in mind, DeVincentis couldn't believe that Stephen Frears was even in the running for directing the film. Their first meeting was in a hotel room in New York, during which Stephen Frears never sat down. "He's a pacer," says DeVincentis.[20] So Frears wound up just pacing around the room while speaking to the boys. Eventually, he leaned against the wall and said, "Right, right. Well this sounds like good fun." That was Frears's ever-so charming way of committing to do the film.

When Frears was told by the boys that the film would be set in Chicago, his initial reaction basically matched a lot of the critics at that time. "Well, that's not a very good idea," Frears recalls telling them.

However, after reading the script, he agreed with Hornby's line of thinking that it didn't matter where it was set. That wasn't the important part of the story.

"You could see that the boys had changed it to suit their age and their taste in music," Frears concluded.[21]

So three years after the option was first made in 1995, it seems like the pieces were finally coming together just as they should. A first draft had already been written when John Cusack and Steve Pink were in Calgary working on *The Jack Bull*. This left DeVincentis to fly to London to work on a new draft of the script, this time with Stephen Frears.

"Stephen wanted to get going on the script," DeVincentis recalls. "And so he said, 'All right, just send the other one,' which was me, to London. It was September of '98. So suddenly, I'm getting on a plane to go to London to be supervised through a draft by one of my all-time heroes."[22]

D.V. was put up at the Halcyon Hotel, which was not too far from Stephen's home. Every morning for about a month, Stephen would visit D.V. at the House Sand Hotel and order up room service. After breakfast, he'd ask questions about the story and have D.V. answer them. Frears would then leave DeVincentis to incorporate his answers into the script, and pop back over at around four or five to see where things were.

One of the biggest hurdles with adapting *High Fidelity* for the screen was figuring out how to tackle the narration. In the book, it's representative of Rob's internal. He is taking you on this journey through his mind as he goes through his day-to-day and tries to sort out his life and see where things had gone wrong in his relationships.

When it came to figuring out how to translate something like that to the screen, that's where it got tricky. As Rob's internal back-and-forth made up so much of the book, to cut it out entirely would obviously be a grave injustice. Yet there are also limitations when you're adapting things for another medium. So it created a challenge that Cusack, Pink, DeVincentis, and Frears had to collaborate on to figure out how to tackle it.

"I'm not a big voice-over guy and I don't like movies that tend to depend upon it," says DeVincentis. "But the prose is so good and so insightful into Rob's character, you don't want to lose it."[23]

In the first draft the boys wrote, they used the voice-over technique. This was done solely as a way to somehow work Hornby's brilliant internal dialogue he created for Rob into the book into the final film. At the time, it seemed like the easiest way to carry things over from one medium to the other.

From the jump, Frears was not a fan of having voice-over for the movie. He simply felt that the ratio would get lost at some point in the process. While working with DeVincentis on the script in London, it was actually his idea to implement direct address, with Cusack speaking to the camera.

DeVincentis was on board with the idea right away. From there, he ran it by Pink, who also felt like it was the right way to go.

Says Pink,

> The first person voice direct-to-camera embodied so much of what we were trying to achieve with the movie and so much of the spirit of Nick Hornby's prose. In the book, it's first person, and there's something to the way that this deeply flawed and charming person is expressing the feeling of everything he's saying, which is a connection that you have when you're reading the fucking book. You have that connection. The reader has that connection with Nick and the character of Rob when you're reading it. So it struck me as absolutely clear that that was essential to do when we were making the movie.[24]

From there, DeVincentis and Pink strategized on how they would sell Cusack on the idea—not that they necessarily believed that he would be opposed to the idea. Rather, they already both recognized that this was the most logical direction to go in. They knew there was no other option that made as much sense. So they wanted to make sure they got the same enthusiastic response from Cusack.

Pink recalls, "We were always like 'If he says no, then fuck us. Goddammit! We don't want to make any other version of the movie anymore. There's only one way to make this movie.'"[25]

Luckily for them, Cusack agreed with DeVincentis and Pink that this was the proper way to go. So that's what it became. Case closed.

As it would turn out, having Cusack directly address the audience allows us to feel an even closer connection to Rob that we would not have otherwise. If you were only hearing the thoughts in his head, you would've felt that there was some sort of barrier between yourself and the character. After all, it's a character that it can occasionally be hard to feel sympathy for.

But when Rob is looking directly at you, it becomes all the easier to relate to him. In those moments, the drawbridge has been lowered. He is more or less exposing every raw nerve he's got within him as he bares his goddamn soul to you. Rob milks that direct address with everything he's got.

Having a performer like John Cusack also makes all the difference in the world. That's because breaking the fourth wall is not an easy thing to do as an actor. When you're breaking the fourth wall, you're asking the audience to come with you down a road that is least taken. As a general rule of thumb, most films would never have a character so much as look directly into the camera let alone talk to you as a narrator.

If you've got an actor who doesn't commit to it 100 percent, it could read as being hackneyed or over the top. Luckily, Cusack approached every direct address with much more realism. It never stopped the momentum. It all fit like a perfect glove. Much like how DeVincentis and Pink initially felt, when you see the film with Rob addressing the audience, you simply cannot imagine it being done any other way.

After about a month of their daily sessions, DeVincentis and Frears flew to Calgary to meet with John Cusack and Steve Pink while they were working on *The Jack Bull*. The four of them went over the new changes and did further work as a group to develop the script. Once everyone got on the same page, that's when things started moving in the right direction and the script truly started taking shape.

Once they were done in Calgary, Frears had some business he had to take care of in Los Angeles. But instead of opting to fly, he insisted that he and DeVincentis take a road trip together. Why? Because Stephen Frears is a big road trip fan. It was a trip that DeVincentis equates to being his own personal version of *My Favorite Year*.

Turns out that no car rental service would rent Frears a car, however, to cross the Canadian border. So instead, Frears and DeVincentis flew on a prop plane to the most northernly point of the United States where you could land a plane, which was Kalispell, Montana.

From there, the duo continued on their American trek, during which DeVincentis recalls that Stephen Frears almost got bit by a rattlesnake at Little Big Horn and the two of them saw *Ronin* in the middle of Wyoming.

"I love those big drives in America," Frears recalls. "We went through Wyoming, we went through Little Big Horn, Jackson Hole, Reno, and Yosemite, which I loved. And Yellowstone. Yellowstone I didn't find so interesting, but Yosemite I thought was wonderful."[26]

As for the script itself, it would go through several changes still—even in the midst of production. The script was more or less always evolving, with an abundance of new script pages—all in different colors—being instituted throughout the process.

"This is the greatest lesson I've ever learned from Frears," says DeVincentis. "The script is never done. You think it's perfect, but you can make it more perfect. You think it has ideas. Well, nothing stands still. Ideas don't stand still. The more you think about them, the better they should form."[27]

The film was well underway in preproduction before a producer came on board. Some movies start with a producer optioning a property. Others start with a screenwriter writing a script on spec. In the case of *High Fidelity*, it started with a music supervisor. So eventually, they realized they needed to bring someone in. Stephen Frears knew just the right team.

Stephen Frears had a long working relationship with producer Tim Bevan. Frears and Bevan first connected in the mid-1980s. At the time, Bevan hadn't produced a film yet when Frears enlisted him to produce his 1985 film, *My Beautiful Laundrette*. From there, they worked together on *Sammy and Rosie Get Laid* and *The Hi-Lo Country*.

In between those two films, Bevan and the company he cofounded, Working Title, built up a solid reputation for themselves in the industry. Naturally, Frears invited Bevan to produce *High Fidelity*.

As for the film's line producer, Stephen tapped Rudd Simmons to fill that role.

Simmons got his start as a producer with Jim Jarmusch, having produced his 1989 short *Coffee and Cigarettes II*. He then followed it up by working as a line producer on Jarmusch's next films, *Mystery Train* and *Night on Earth*. Following his work with Jarmusch, Simmons also produced *The Night We Never Met*; *New Jersey Drive*; *Dead Man Walking*; and *Boys*.

Simmons first got involved with Frears through Tim Bevan, whom Simmons had worked with numerous times prior. While working on *Dead Man Walking*, Simmons was offered to executive produce *The Hi-Lo Country*, which is where he first got introduced to Stephen Frears.

"Tim and Stephen had known each other since the very beginning when they were working on music videos together," recalls Simmons. "And then, of course, they made a couple of movies together. So there was a comfort level there."[28]

After forming a good working relationship with Frears on *The Hi-Lo Country*, Simmons was asked to produce *High Fidelity*.

Starting in 1985, Oliver Stapleton was Stephen Frears's go-to cinematographer. They had worked together on *My Beautiful Launderette*; *Prick Up Your Ears*; *Sammy and Rosie Get Laid*; *The Grifters*; *Hero*; *The Van*; and *The Hi-Lo Country*. But for *High Fidelity*, Frears would need to turn to a new cinematographer.

Seamus McGarvey was in his late twenties and had worked on a series of shorts, music videos, and feature films. In 1999, he was at the Edinburgh Film Festival with Tim Roth's first—and to-date only—film as a director, *The War Zone*. Seamus went into a bar and sat down for a pint seated next to a man he did not know. That man he was sitting next to was Stephen Frears, naturally.

"We got talking," McGarvey recalls of their first meeting.

> I said, "Why are you here?" And he said, "Oh, I've come to see this film. It's Tim Roth's film." And I said, "Well, I am actually the cinematographer of that." And he said, "Oh really? Well, my fucking cinematographer has just left me. Do you want to come and shoot a film in Chicago?"[29]

Frears offered McGarvey the job without having seen his work. Following their conversation, McGarvey went with Frears to the screening of *The War Zone*. After the film ended, in true Frears fashion, all he said was "Yeah, come and shoot this film with me."

Two weeks later, McGarvey found himself on a tech scout in Chicago for his first-ever American studio movie. All of this because he had the urge to go get a pint at the Edinburgh Film Festival and by chance picked the right person to sit next to.

"I almost felt throughout the film slightly on the backfoot or I was an imposter in some way," McGarvey recalls. "I was young, I was in my twenties, and it really was a huge opportunity to shoot a Hollywood studio movie with such big stars, like John Cusack."[30]

"I never looked back," McGarvey continues. "It was like the big slingshot moment in my career. I put on the slipper and it fit."[31]

"Frears had total confidence in Seamus, and so did we," says DeVincentis. "Seamus hit the ground running with such authority. He had such a great spirit to work with. He was so positive. He rolled with stress so well."[32]

It's the sort of dream-like scenario that every budding artist dreams of finding themselves in. One imagines that Frears had made a conscious decision to surround himself with younger talent for

this particular project, such as Seamus McGarvey as well as DeVincentis, Pink, and Cusack.

"I think that Stephen surrounded himself with young people
because he felt that there was a zeitgeist that he wanted to tap into,
which is the world of the film," says Simmons. "And maybe that's one
of the reasons why the picture works, because there's always a new
generation that's going through the challenges."[33]

With that, in the fall of 1998, they started location scouting in
Chicago.

4

Sweet Home Chicago

Back in Chicago, Wicker Park was a world that the three screenwriters had a direct link to, as they had all lived in Wicker Park in the 1990s. DeVincentis recalls living right down the street from what would become one of the film's locations, the Double Door. This was before it was the Double Door and back when it was a run-down ranchero bar. Most of DeVincentis's time back then was hanging at another filming location—Lounge Ax—or a nearby bar he'd frequent, Dreamers.

They had lived there before it ever became gentrified. Today, Wicker Park is in some ways unrecognizable if you compare it with the film. Even by the time they made the film in 1999, gentrification had begun rearing its head as things were already starting to change rapidly since the time they had lived there.

When you read the script, you can't help but feel the intense affinity they had for Wicker Park. This was an important part of their lives, and it made its way into what they were doing with *High Fidelity*.

"It was a place you'd go if you wanted to be an artist," Pink says about the neighborhood. "The story of gentrification is the story of artists looking for affordable places to live. That was Wicker Park. So we happened to feel the growth of that neighborhood happen around us in the few years that we lived there before we moved to L.A."[1]

"It just had so much character," adds the film's unit production manager Billy Higgins. "Every place you went was just kind of bleeding with that. And it was a hip scene. It was an artistic scene. From art, painting, literature, and photography, as well as the music joints."[2]

During this time especially, one of the things that Wicker Park was most renowned for was its indie music scene. If you were looking to break into music in Chicago in the 1990s, Wicker Park was the place you had to be. On any given night, you could see some of the best bands the Midwest had to offer playing the Double Door, Lounge Ax, or a variety of other alt-venues that were scattered throughout the immediate area.

"We were always striving for authentic places," Pink says about finding the right places to feature in the film. "Things obviously felt more authentic to us when we actually had inhabited them to watch bands and play music."[3]

There are two core music venues that are featured in *High Fidelity*. The first is Lounge Ax. This is the venue in the film where Rob sees the character Marie play the Peter Frampton cover "Baby I Love Your Way," leading to the now-classic line "Is that Peter fucking Frampton?"

Lounge Ax—which was located in Lincoln Park directly across the street from the record label Wrax Trax—opened in 1987. In 1989, a woman named Sue Miller started managing the place. Miller wound up getting married at the club in the 1990s to Jeff Tweedy from Wilco.

While there were many great music venues springing up during that era in Chicago, this was one that had a lot of really special qualities going for it. For anyone interested in the music scene during the 1990s, Lounge Ax was in many ways your home away from home. Hell, there's people who spent more time there than in their actual homes.

"Lounge Ax was a unique venue," recalls DeVincentis.

> It really was an incubator and a cradle for a lot of Chicago alternative rock and roll in the '90s. It was always on the verge of going out of business. The list of people who played there was insane. Somebody who was just hanging out there and was occasionally doing like really fucking insane stand-up shit there was Fred Armisen.[4]

"It was really experimental and supportive," Armisen recalls about the Wicker Park scene from that era. While Armisen himself was not involved in the film, he has crisp memories of the scene and of all the locations where the characters in the film spent time, as well as the places where those who made the film hung out. His band, *Trenchmouth*, was a notable staple of the scene at the time.[5]

"Lounge Ax felt like the center," Armisen continues.

> Anyone from any scene would also play Lounge Axe. And it just seemed like common ground. If you looked at the bookings, everyone played there. I think Lounge Axe did a good job of making the bands feel at home and promoting the shows.[6]

Shooting at Lounge Ax was an obvious choice. This was the type of place where Rob, Barry, and Dick would actually go to hang out after work. That's because it was the type of place that the people that DeVincentis, Pink, and Cusack knew would go hang out.

Lounge Ax being featured in the film was also good for the venue, and not just in terms of shining a spotlight on it. Lounge Ax was one of those places that seemed like it was always on the verge of closing down. So it was a good way to help feed money into it in an attempt to help keep the doors open for just a little while longer.

The other music venue that you see in the film is the Double Door. This is where the record-release party is held at the end of the film. The Double Door was a newer venue at the time, having opened in 1994, and therefore it didn't quite have the same prestige that Lounge Ax had on the scene.

Despite how new it was, the Double Door was nevertheless a good place to go see bands play. Some of the various artists and bands who walked through the doors were the Smashing Pumpkins; Liz Phair; Cheap Trick; Rise Against; the Killers; and Sonic Youth. Hell, even the Rolling Stones did a concert at the Double Door.

However, the previous incarnation of the Double Door was a lot less hip. According to Higgins, it was rundown and "smelled like urine and throw-up." During this time period, the bar had a sign out front advertising a "commuter special." This was where businessmen could go get a beer and a shot for $1.85 between 6 a.m. and 8 a.m.[7]

"That was a great place," Armisen says of the Double Door. "They did a good job of getting their sound system together, the location was really good. And it was just like an added venue where more bands could play at. The location was great."[8]

It was, indeed, a great location, right in the heart of everything in Wicker Park. Located on Milwaukee Avenue, even the vintage Double Doors Liquors sign outside the venue became a trademark of the neighborhood.

One thing you'll notice when you watch *High Fidelity* is just how many different restaurants and bars we see the characters hanging out in. When you watch most films, they'll have one central location that is a hub for those characters. In *High Fidelity,* you get a little bit of everything.

Much like how they placed the characters in a neighborhood that fit who they were, they did the same with the places they would frequent. For instance, the restaurant we see Laura and her friend Liz eating in is Smith and Wollensky, a steakhouse located on State

Street. Being that they're both attorneys, they belonged in a place that felt a bit more upscale.

For Sarah Kendrew, one of the various ex-girlfriends that Rob revisits in the film, they wanted to find a bar that looked a lot more boring and uninteresting. This would reflect some of her plainer character traits—or at least what Rob perceived her character traits to be.

Then, of course, there's Rob. Yes, we see him hanging out all over the place, from Lounge Ax to the Rainbo Club to the Double Door. But if there were a place that we could picture Rob going to hang out in on a regular basis, it would be the Green Mill Cocktail Lounge.

The Green Mill is featured in the film as where Rob tells the audience about Laura's pregnancy; admits his infidelity; reveals the large sum of money he's borrowed; and tells Laura that he's "kind of sort of maybe looking around for someone else." In short, this is where we see Rob open up even more to the audience, telling us, "I am a fucking asshole."

The Green Mill is just the kind of place that Rob would go hang out to escape the world of Championship Vinyl and the crowded music scene sometimes.

"I loved going to the Green Mill because it was a place that was bigger than ourselves," recalls Pink.

> First of all, it was a really cool bar to go to. Secondly, it wasn't always crowded. Going to Rainbo or Lounge Ax or Double Door, you had to be in a certain mood to be around a lot of people. You could pretty much count on the Green Mill feeling like a place you could have a drink and still be a beautiful environment.[9]

Before *High Fidelity*, the Green Mill was most notably seen on screen in *Thief* as the bar that James Caan's character often visits and that we see him burning down at the end of the movie.

But the bar actually has a rich history within both Chicago as well as pop culture. The venue is renowned for both its jazz and poetry performances. The Green Mill is home to the Uptown Poetry Slam on Sunday nights, the longest running poetry slam in the country. But it's also notable for its history of mob connections.

This is something alluded to on screen in *High Fidelity* if you look hard enough. As we first pan the bar, we see a sign on the piano that says, "Al Capone Drank Here Often."

"Al Capone didn't control the entire city," says DeVincentis. "Al Capone controlled the South Side. As a result, he didn't like to party on the South Side because it was work. He liked to party on the North Side. So he loved partying at the Green Mill."[10]

One of the most notable aspects of the Green Mill is an underground tunnel that was built specifically for Capone. There was a trap door behind the bar that could be used to go into an underground tunnel that spanned that entire block and would allow Capone the opportunity to escape from anyone who might be looking for him.

Lounge Axe was directly across the street from the famous Biograph Theater. Built in 1915, the theater has a long history in its own right, having started off as a movie house before eventually becoming a theater. But it's also notable for being the place where John Dillinger got shot.

While standing outside Lounge Axe during production, DeVincentis told Frears of the theater's history.

DeVincentis recalls,

> I pointed across the street to the Biograph theater, to the little alley next to it. And I said, "Stephen see that alley?" "Yes." "That's the alley where they shot John Dillinger to death." He's like, "What?" "Yeah. And you know what happened? His fucking girlfriend tipped him off. She tipped the cops off and that's how they caught him and shot him dead in that alley." And he's

like, "Well why isn't that in the script? Put it in. We're shooting that!" And it's in the movie.[11]

This, of course, wouldn't be the first time that Chicago would stand front and center in the world of Hollywood. In fact, the city had a long history of being represented in film going back to the 1920s. From 1980 until the early 1990s, there was a long stretch where film productions were totally commonplace—sort of a new golden age of production for the city.

This was after a period that lasted over two decades when very few films were shot in Chicago.

During his twenty-one-year tenure as mayor of Chicago, Richard J. Daley was none too keen on most film productions coming through town. There're multiple theories as far as why this would be. Some say a lot of people in Chicago didn't want films to come in that could "make the city look bad"—especially those that would be highlighting Chicago's gangster roots. Noted film critic Roger Ebert, who wrote for the *Chicago Sun-Times*, suggested that it was actually a result of *Medium Cool*, which incorporated a lot of footage from the 1968 Democratic Convention. Reportedly Daley was none-too-pleased with how the footage made Chicago—and perhaps most importantly Daley himself—look.[12]

After *Medium Cool*, all approval for filming reportedly had to go through Daley, who denied pretty much everything. Any exceptions you might have seen during this time period were almost always shot guerilla style without permits. There were some of those, as a lot of no budget B-movies fell under the radar. But by and large, there wasn't much going on in terms of production in Chicago.

Says Chicago film historian Adam Carston,

Whatever the reason was that Daley didn't let people in, it almost doesn't matter because the big deal was that there wasn't a film office. If you look at New York, one of the reasons why they had so many films in the late '60s, early '70s filmed in and around New York, was because they established a film office that made it much easier to shoot in the city.[13]

This trend continued until 1979. Things changed three years after Daley's death when John Belushi approached Mayor Jane Byrne about filming *The Blues Brothers* there.

Belushi had his heart set on filming it in his hometown. In fact, he pledged to donate $200,000 of his own money to local orphanages in exchange for permission to take over Chicago for filming. But what sealed the deal was the idea of having a car drive through Daley Plaza, named after the man who never would've allowed such an act to take place.

Belushi was not too sure of how Byrne would react to this and, according to Byrne herself, seemed to be expecting her to say no. However Byrne—who faced staunch opposition from supporters of Daley on the campaign trail—was amused by the idea and gave it the greenlight.[14]

"I've always heard that she got some level of blowback for them driving through Daley Plaza," says Carston. "It was like a pretty new building. It was supposed to be a tribute to the former mayor. So I don't think some of the Daley loyalists were necessarily into that kind of deconstruction."[15]

That is how Chicago became a viable location for film shoots for a period. During this period, a series of 1980s and early 1990s films all graced the Windy City. These films included *Risky Business*; *Adventures in Babysitting*; *The Untouchables*; *Thief*; *The Color of Money*; *The Fugitive*; *Candyman*; *Backdraft*; *Ordinary People*; *The Hunter*; and *About Last Night*—which Steve Pink would direct a remake of in 2014.

Most notably, John Hughes was a big source of bringing productions to Chicago. Pretty much every film he made in the 1980s was filmed there including *Vacation*; *Sixteen Candles*; *The Breakfast Club*; *Ferris Bueller's Day Off*; *Weird Science*; *Uncle Buck*; *Planes, Trains, and Automobiles*; *Home Alone*; and *Only the Lonely*. If there was ever a production boom in the city, this was it.

However, by the mid-1990s, it seemed like there was less and less production taking place in a city that, only years before, boasted multiple films being shot any given year. By this point, it was becoming more and more expensive to film in Chicago, which meant that the studios were less likely to want to foot the bill for it.

But for all Cusack, Pink, and DeVincentis were concerned, there would be—and could be—no substitute. It *had* to be Chicago.

"We were very blessed to have the support of the studio at a time when it wasn't that cheap to go to Chicago to shoot a movie of our dreams," Pink reflects. "We fought to shoot it in Chicago. We wrote it for Chicago, we were able to create the world of this movie through our own eyes, basically."[16]

For the trio, shooting in Chicago was a homecoming of sorts. At this stage in their lives, all three were living out in Hollywood, coming hot off the success of their first film as screenwriters. Getting to film in Chicago not only afforded the project an authenticity but it allowed the boys to go home to make exactly the movie they had set out to make. This was a movie that, in so many ways, was a true love letter to their city.

In the fall of '98, location scouting began in Chicago. DeVincentis, Pink, and Cusack knew just how important it was to have the film showcase the places that they themselves and the people they knew would actually be hanging out at. DeVincentis, in particular, took on the role of making sure there was that level of detail and accuracy in every spot they scouted.

"I was really, really excited about sinking this into the Chicago that I knew," says DeVincentis.

And that meant taking Stephen and the production designer around to the record stores that I bought my records at, and still did at that time, and modeling the record store on that record store. I also brought them to apartments of my friends. I took those guys into so many different houses and apartments to show them what average people who were going to Lounge Ax lived like.[17]

"When we were looking for locations, it was about authenticity," echoes McGarvey.

I think Frears has an incredible anchor on humans' feet on the ground. And often, filmmakers can get quite lofty with their cinematic aspirations, which is good for certain projects. But when you're talking about the human condition, sometimes you need to keep your feet on the ground.[18]

But there was one integral piece of the puzzle, sort of the meat of the entire film, that was all depending on one location. This was a location that had to be so absolutely perfect that production couldn't afford to mess it up—a set piece so important that if it weren't exact, any credibility that the film would have had would be lost for good: the record store.

The exteriors of Championship Vinyl were filmed at Honore and Milwaukee. Of course, right from the jump it looks like the type of record shop you'd actually go out of your way to go to. In addition to looking the part, however, it seems to be the sort of place where you'd find a store like Championship Vinyl if it were to actually exist.

While, of course, no records were ever actually sold there, the set decoration did stay up for at least ten years after production wrapped. Today, if you go there looking for Rob, Barry, or Dick—or for some ungodly reason you're on a quest to find a copy of "I Just

Called to Say I Love You" for your daughter—you'll instead find the trendy bicycle shop, Ralpha.

In the script, the store is described this way.

> More light might penetrate the windows if there weren't so many record-release posters taped to them. A dusty narrow corridor clad in burlap and shag rug. On the walls are bagged 45s you will never hear unless you commit your life to the losing proposition of listening to every noodling of Jah Wobble and Glen Glenn and other people you've never heard of.[19]

The interior of the record store, however, was not filmed on location. It was all done on a soundstage in Chicago. That wasn't always going to be the case, though.

Initially, Stephen Frears had wanted to film the entire movie on location, including the record-store scenes. Most directors tend to not want to shoot on location due to the limitations that goes along with doing so. On location, you can't move walls and shelves around like you can on a set. You are pretty much locked into what's already there, with very little wiggle room.

However, Frears always looks for any opportunity he can get to shoot on location. He wants to make sure it's as close to looking as realistic as possible.

The hunt to find an actual record store to shoot in was challenging. Every single record store seemed to have the same problem, which was the overall layout. Your average record store is designed like a little shoebox, with records and shelves crammed into the tiniest spaces imaginable. This alone would've severely impacted how you'd set up your shots, as well as limit how many people you could fit into the space.

Against all odds, they finally managed to find one they all liked and one that had the right amount of space. As soon as they walked in,

Frears started getting really excited. "This is it," he proudly proclaimed. "I don't know what it was," recalls Simmons. "It was the vibe that he was picking up. But the problem was that the city bus ran directly in front of the store, and it would have been incredibly noisy and very, very disruptive to us to try and work there."[20]

However, some remnants of this specific store are seen in the film. Instead of shooting on location, they took measurements of the store and used the same layout—complete with the glass in the backroom—in their own record-store set. It was as close as you could get to having the perfect record store.

Shortly before production began, the production designer who was working on the film, Thérèse DePrez, had to resign from the project due to health problems. A replacement had to be found immediately. This meant that whoever would take her place would have a super-fast turnaround if *High Fidelity* would still be able to start rolling on time.

Just three to four weeks before production, David Chapman received a phone call from Higgins saying *High Fidelity* needed someone fast. There was only about five to six weeks left before production, so they needed someone who could jump into action on a moment's notice.

Having someone as accomplished as Chapman involved was certainly key to this timeline. As a production designer, Chapman had worked on films like *Dirty Dancing*; *Mystic Pizza*; *Last Exit to Brooklyn*; *Grumpy Old Men*; and *Simon Birch*.

Luckily for Chapman, he wouldn't be starting from scratch. There was already a team assembled, and DePrez had done some preliminary work before she was forced to drop out. Nevertheless, Chapman says it's not an experience he would ever like to repeat.

"I knew that they would move those record bins nine thousand times when they were in there," says Chapman, reflecting on how the set was constructed. "Because they'd always be in the way. So I put all of those on wheels so we could open up that space."[21]

When it came to record stores in movies, there had only been a handful over the years. When you think about the representation of record stores in movies, there're a few different ones that might come to mind. Maybe it's the record store from *Pretty in Pink* where we watch Jon Cryer pull off a now borderline-iconic Otis Redding impression. Or maybe it's the glass-mirror-maze record store of the dystopian future where Alex picks up the two women in *A Clockwork Orange*.

However, if you were to think about any other film that was set almost entirely in a record store, there's a pretty good chance that *Empire Records* might immediately come to mind.

Empire Records was released in 1995 and boasted a cast that consisted of Liv Tyler, Renee Zellweger, Anthony LaPaglia, Debi Mazar, Rory Cochrane, Ethan Randall, Johnny Whitworth, Robin Tunney, and Maxwell Caulfield.

Unlike *High Fidelity* where the plot is hinged more on the relationships with the record store merely being a backdrop, *Empire Records* focuses on a plot that's actually not too far removed from what Scott Rosenberg was hoping to do with *High Fidelity*. In the film, which takes place over the course of one day, we see a small independent record store where the employees are doing everything they can to stop it from being bought out by a mega-chain of stores.

The store itself feels more like what Hollywood executives who had never stepped foot in an actual record store outside the trendiest parts of Los Angeles in the 1990s might have cooked up. The record store in *Empire Records* feels far more spacious than your typical independent record shop, complete with a spiral staircase toward the back. How many of your mom-and-pop record shops have two stories, let alone a finely crafted spiral staircase that connects them?

It's clear when you look at the record store in *Empire Records* that the target demographic was teens and those in their early twenties because that's who worked in the store.

Oddly enough, there is a link that sort-of ties together *Empire Records* and *High Fidelity*: D.V. DeVincentis.

DeVincentis actually auditioned for the part of the manager that eventually went to Anthony LaPaglia. As he left the audition, the film's director Allan Moyle told DeVincentis, "You have to be in this movie."

"He had me do a table reading of it," adds DeVincentis. "Then afterwards, he told me I was great and he couldn't wait 'til we were all on set making the movie, and I just never heard from him again."[22]

In basically every way, however, what you see on-screen in *Empire Records* couldn't be more different from the world of Championship Vinyl.

In *High Fidelity*, things feel a lot more drab and depressing. Throughout the film, Rob laments about the store numerous times, mentioning the only people who shop there are those who go out of their way to shop there. That means that it had to look a bit more desolate, as if it's the sort of place that's effectively holding Rob back in life. The store should be cluttered with band posters and boxes that give off an unorganized chaos sort of vibe. That's the sort of thing you'd find in your average Chicago record shop.

Another person who took the record store very seriously was DeVincentis, with the help of his friend Dan Koretzky. Koretzky was not only one of DeVincentis's closest friends, he was also the founder of Drag City, one of the biggest independent record labels in Chicago.

Koretzky said, "I think I might have been the only obsessive music fan they knew/took pity on/subsequently found a good use for?"[23]

"Dan has always been my greatest source of music to listen to," says DeVincentis. "If I need new stuff to listen to, I ask him and that's how I get turned on to a whole wealth of stuff."[24]

"He just knows all the details," adds Armisen, who became good friends with Koretzky during his time in Chicago and even wound up putting out some records on the Drag City label later on. "When we talk about music, there's things he notices that not everyone notices. And that's what I like about hanging out with him."[25]

DeVincentis had initially offered to make Koretzky an associate producer on the film, given how much he knew he could contribute. Koretzky declined any such credit but made his resources and expertise available whenever called upon.

Chapman openly admits that he is not a music person. So he went up to DeVincentis and Pink and told them that not only did he not know anything about music, he didn't even know enough to try and fake it. Therefore, he encouraged the boys to just tell him what they wanted to see in there, and he would make it happen.

DeVincentis, especially, took this task to heart. He labored over that record store, creating the most ideal record store one could ever possibly imagine. Every aspect of what you see in there was meticulously crafted to create a place where you could actually envision it being somewhere local music obsessives would want to spend all of their time, as well as their money. You could watch *High Fidelity* ten times in a row and still discover new things in Championship Vinyl that you hadn't noticed before.

Says DeVincentis, "I was super specific and micromanaging about both and how they looked. The signage and the posters and the stereo and the everything."[26]

Finding enough records to fill an entire record store convincingly proved to be a challenge all on its own. The production team had to find a large sum of records, all at a decent price. Fortunately, they managed to find a local record store that was going out of business and managed to buy up their entire inventory to fill up the set with.

Both DeVincentis and Koretzky were horrified, however, when they got to the set and saw that the records were entirely made up of Christian and Barbra Streisand records.

"I, at that point, remembered that the record store that the set decorator cleared out was a Christian record store," DeVincentis recalls. "And all of these records are old Christian music records and spoken word and sermon."[27]

"I warned that if the camera stopped moving for a second, all credibility in the store might be lost," Koretzky remembered. "So we quickly ran to Dusty Groove records in Chicago and bought A–Z records by people almost as cool as Babs to sit at the very front of the racks."[28]

DeVincentis was also super intent on the timeline of the store. He knew that since we see the record store over the course of an extended period of time, the same records aren't always going to be on the rack. So he created a chart that he and Koretzky used to determine what would be a realistic cycle for the store. It was all about the details, even down to the minutia.

"I drove the set decorator crazy by creating an actual timeline we had to stick to, even though we were shooting out of chronology," DeVincentis says. "It was like this intense, insane graph that we had to stick to keep the continuity of the record faces."[29]

"He would decide what records might have been sold and what records would still be there," says Pink. "He would go around doing that before every shot. The authenticity was super important to all of us."[30]

When you're shooting something like a record store, practically every single item you see on-screen becomes a clearance nightmare. If a character holds up a record on-screen, that record has to be cleared. For instance, production would have to clear *Blonde on Blonde* or a French LP pressing of *Captain Beefheart* because both records are actually visible on-screen. The same applied to any of the show posters you'd see scattered throughout the shop. All of that required clearances.

Thankfully, the same rules did not apply to every single record that lined the shelves. If you have a large quantity of images in a certain frame—such as twenty or thirty records—then you would not need to have them cleared. Essentially, this would be considered a crowd shot. If you are singling in on a specific record, however, then you would need to have it cleared. This is why the amount of times you see a character physically holding up a record is extremely limited.

In addition to helping DeVincentis with the record store, Koretzky also played an integral part in the film finding its new final act.

The book ends with Laura booking Marie to do an in-person concert in Championship Vinyl, as well as featuring the journalist who comes to interview Rob and serves as his last temptation. At that moment, the question is *Will Rob remain faithful to Laura and commit himself to their future? Or will he fall back into old habits, starting with making the journalist a mix-tape?*

The latter is his signature move. It was also a classic move for music obsessives of that era. What good is having great taste in music if you can't share it with the rest of the world? Making a mix-tape afforded you that opportunity, and you got to introduce your friends and family to cool music in the process.

Of course, making a mix-tape for a woman you were interested in was also par for the course. Sharing a collection of songs you thought she'd like was a smooth way to show that you were thinking about her. Just as much as it could be a kind gesture to introduce your tastes to someone else, it could also help win your way into someone's heart. It was a real win-win scenario.

However, that ending was not in the first draft of the script DeVincentis, Pink, and Cusack turned in.

Instead, the boys ended the first draft with the so-called happier ending of Rob and Laura getting back together and leaving out the entire subplot of the journalist. We don't see Rob try to figure out what the next stage of his life is. What happens after Rob and Laura reconnect is left up to the audience's imagination. This, however, did not sit well with Frears.

"No, you have to put that in the script," Frears told the boys, according to DeVincentis. "That's the point. You have to show him fail again, and he's finally so frustrated with himself that he finally fucking gets it and commits himself to Laura in a real way."[31]

Eventually, they realized Frears was right, and that ending made it into the film. The film's screenwriters, however, had an idea that would take the film in a different direction than how the book ended.

DeVincentis, in particular, was very intrigued by the line that existed between those who create and those who are critical and what it'd be like if someone who was a critic set out to create something. This seemed tailor-made for Rob, who we see for most of the film as being passionate about music, or at least the music that *he* likes. But we never really see him having the ambition to go out and do something about it himself.

For the film, it was decided that Rob would take the next step in his life by starting up an indie record label. This was born out of having watched Dan Koretzky do just that with Drag City. Drag City, as DeVincentis recalls, was born in the apartment they both shared back in 1987.

"There was a day when Dan decided he was going to put out his first single and it was Royal Trux actually," says DeVincentis. "That was a big deal. And it took him from a spectator to someone taking part in the process. So to me, that was something I thought would be great for Rob."[32]

With the locations, script, director, key crew members, ending, and non–Barbra Streisand or Christian records firmly in place, it was time to find the cast.

5

Put It All on Black

If you've ever stepped foot inside a record store, you know people like Barry and Dick. Barry and Dick—or as Rob calls them, "the musical moron twins"—work for Rob in Championship Vinyl. Both have an encyclopedic knowledge of records and music in general. Dick is happy to introduce you to some music you haven't heard before. Barry will just chastise you for not having the same taste as him. Both clearly know a lot more about music than you do.

In the world of *High Fidelity*, Barry is clearly the comic relief. As the over-the-top know-it-all, he always seems to be in direct conflict with either Rob or Dick, given just how borderline obnoxious he can be at times. Much of Rob is internalized, from his rage to his reflection. Dick is more meek and soft-spoken than Barry.

Barry is the ultimate smartass who has no qualms about telling you your music tastes suck, should he be offended by them. But the character of Barry has to also have enough redeeming qualities so you can believe that Rob would put up with his nonsense for as long as he has. There's an endearing passion that brews in Barry. The endearing nature of this passion is so strong, in fact, that he can back up—or at least get away with—the music snobbery that looms on the surface. You know that there are redeemable qualities that lay underneath his brash demeanor.

For Hornby, Barry was a character that was very easy and a lot of fun to write. It all sort of generated organically. Here is a guy who says funny and stupid things throughout the entire book but then manages to back it all up in the third act by proving all the naysayers wrong and having some solid musical chops.

But for an author, that's as far as it goes. He didn't have to think about who could play a part like Barry because he didn't have to find someone to play Barry. It stayed within the page.

"When I first met D.V. and John," recalls Nick Hornby, "I said, 'I don't know who you're going to get for that guy.' Because I thought *He's not a real person.* And D.V. said, 'Well, I know that guy!'"[1]

Cusack, Pink, and DeVincentis first met Jack Black in Los Angeles where they were all part of Tim Robbins's the Actor's Gang.

As Pink remembers, "D.V. and I did this show called *Carnage* a year later. And then I had to go back to Berkeley. I'm not sure if they extended right away or they remounted it, but Jack Black replaced me."[2]

Jack Black's brand of humor was visible even then. They got to witness the birth of Tenacious D, as Black and Kyle Gass would play on the second floor of the theater in East Santa Monica after the show wrapped for the night. Just the mere mention of Jack Black would elicit laughter out of the trio. They watched "Jack be Jack" everywhere from up onstage to late night hangs at Canter's Deli. As far as they were concerned, he was already a star. The rest of the world just had to catch up and discover him, too.

It was Robbins who first put Black on the big screen, where he played a memorable part in Robbins's film *Bob Roberts* in 1992. However, their professional relationship predated that by about ten years. When Jack Black was eleven years old, he did a play that was directed by Robbins, who was fresh out of UCLA at the time. The play was *Inside Eddie Pinstock*. Black and Robbins would of course go on to work together many times after this.

Following his big leap into the world of cinema, Black started popping up both on TV and in the movies where he had roles in

Demolition Man; *The Cable Guy*; *The Neverending Story III*; *Waterworld*; *The X-Files*; *Mars Attacks!*; *Cradle Will Rock*; and *Enemy of the State*. Simultaneously, Tenacious D was just starting to gain some underground traction after appearing on *Mr. Show w/Bob and Dave*. This eventually lead to the D getting their own HBO series in 1997. But even as things were taking off, Black still needed to have a breakout role. The role of Barry was just what he needed.

"When we were talking about casting for Barry," recalls Pink, "I know that there were other names out there and I don't know how Jack's name came up, but we were like, 'We've got to get Jack Black to do this. He is the perfect person to play this role.'"[3]

"I already knew that he was a great musician and singer and a great comic actor who was about to explode," Cusack has stated. "But I felt like I had this secret weapon because no one really knew that he could rock that much. So the book was perfect and I thought *This is the perfect role for him*."[4]

Yes, there were indeed other names that either auditioned for the role or were at least considered for it. Names on the shortlist included David Arquette, Mike O'Malley, David Cross, Zak Orth, Zack Galifianakis, Dave Foley, Jason Lee, Sam Rockwell, Liev Schreiber, James LeGros, and Philip Seymour Hoffman. Some of the names, such as Hoffman, were also considered for the other member of the record store's motley crew, Dick. However, Stephen Frears admits he couldn't quite decide if Hoffman was better suited as Barry or Dick.

To cast the film, Frears enlisted Victoria Thomas. Thomas had previously worked with Frears and Cusack together on *The Grifters*. Additionally, she had worked on various other projects over the years starting in 1984 with *Repo Man*. She followed this up with *Sid and Nancy* as well as *Beverly Hills Cop I*; *Edward Scissorhands*; *Indecent Proposal*; *The Piano*; *Ed Wood*; *Tin Cup*; *Mars Attacks!*; *Con Air*; *Bulworth*; *Enemy of the State*; and with Frears again on *The Hi-Lo Country*.

Like Cusack, DeVincentis, and Pink, she had known Jack Black through all the times that he'd auditioned for her over the years. She felt that he was perfect for the role of Barry.

In the novel, the part reads as being—as Stephen Frears recalls—"a lot more aggressive." When he first read the script, which more or less somewhat tones down Barry's more aggressive tendencies, Jack Black could see a number of similarities between himself and the character in the script.[5]

"He's kind of a scraggily vagabond," Black recalls. "I could relate to that. His lifestyle of kind of a Bohemian ne'er-do-well. He's a trickster. He's a class clown at the record store. And he'll push a joke too far, all the way up to the level where he's about to get slapped. Or he actually does get slapped."[6]

Unsurprisingly, though, when they floated the name by Frears, he was unfamiliar with Jack Black. "I said, 'Who should play this part?' And the boys said, 'Jack Black.' And I said, 'Who's he?' And he came to see me and I said, 'Well, you'll be fine.'"[7]

As DeVincentis recalls of the meeting,

> Jack comes in, he sits down, and Stephen looks at me and goes, "This is him?" I go, "This is him." And Stephen looks him up and down and goes, "Alright. You'll do." Imagine Jack looking around confused. "Excuse me? What?" And Stephen was like, "You're fine. Great. We'll have you." And Jack's like, "You want me to read or anything?" And he's like, "Absolutely not. You're fine." And Jack gets up and leaves. I was kind of nervous because I knew it was right, but didn't he want to know?[8]

So Jack Black got the role on the spot. He then wound up turning it down.

"I got the script and I read it," remembers Black, reflecting on his surprising decision to turn the part down.

And I was just worried that, at the time, *Tenacious D* had a full head of steam, and we were getting great crowds and were playing to big houses. And I had, in my mind, a legitimate rock-and-roll career, separate from film and television, that I wanted to protect. And to do a movie about music, playing sort of a music critic and talking about some of my heroes like Kurt Cobain, just all those elements made me nervous about messing with this thing that was my own little crown jewel of my life and career up to that moment. I was hesitant to fuck with that.[9]

Victoria Thomas, got a call from Jack Black's agent, Sharon Jackson. The gist of the message was clear. Thomas was informed that Jack didn't want to do the film. She then got frustrated with Jackson for not trying to calm him down and help alleviate his fears. Jackson told her, "Well, it's Jack. This is what he wants to do."[10]

As Cusack saw it, he might have been frightened by the scope of it. While he was obviously no stranger to acting by this point, this would be inarguably the biggest role he had yet to take on in the film world. Cusack also did his best to try and alleviate his fears, assuring him that with the team that they'd assembled, he didn't have anything to worry about.[11]

In hindsight, Jack Black agrees that fear was a factor. "If I'm really being honest with myself, I was terrified of failing. I was terrified of being bad in this movie and also terrified of working with Stephen Frears."[12]

Much like DeVincentis, Jack Black was a huge fan of Stephen Frears. He recalls having seen *Dangerous Liaisons* twelve times because he was obsessed with John Malkovich and wanted to be just like him. But then the idea of working with Frears started getting into his head. Black started questioning whether or not he was good enough. That was another big reason why Black wanted to take himself out of the running. It was all based on fear.

As Frears recalls,

> I got a message saying that Jack Black doesn't want to do the film. I said, "Don't be so stupid. Have him call me." So Jack called me. I said, "What's the matter?" And he said, "Well, you didn't make me audition. When I audition, it makes me realize that I can do it," or words to that effect. So I said, "Well fine. As it happens, I'm coming to Los Angeles next week. So you can come and audition for the part." So he went from having the part to being up to the part.[13]

"I told him about my fears," Black adds.

> And he just thought it was funny that I was passing. Because it was obvious to him and to anyone in my life that this was a no-brainer. And it would be a huge mistake to bail on it for any reason other than I just didn't like it. And that was not the case. I loved the script and I love Stephen and I realized that I was just passing on it out of fear. And that was not a good reason. And so I said, "Okay, I'll do it."[14]

Later on, Frears finally asked Black why he was actually pushing back. According to Frears, Black said, "I earned a good living keeping my head down. And you were asking me to stick my head up."[15]

At the end of the day, there's a great deal of irony in Jack Black passing on the film that brought him as much attention as *High Fidelity* did. He was clearly always going to break out. Even when you watch some of his earliest performances, such as playing Matthew Broderick's best friend in *The Cable Guy*, you are immediately drawn to him whenever he is on-screen. On the screen he has this ability to have you completely buy into whatever he is selling through his physical mannerisms, his facial characteristics—such as his wild eyebrows—and his overall demeanor.

He received no better opportunity to break out than *High Fidelity*. It's akin to watching somebody being shot out of a canon. The raw electricity that passes through him can be seen from miles away. And it's that very intensity that allowed him to walk away with the film.

But despite Black taking things from 0 to 60 on-screen at a moment's notice, he still had bouts with anxiety and doubt over just how good he was in the film. Thus, he adopted a mantra to keep him in the zone at all times.

"I was freaking out," he admits, with the anxieties now twenty years in the rearview mirror but still as vivid as they were back in the day. "I was not used to this getting a big part in a Hollywood movie. I had some little breaks here and there, and mainly my big break was Tenacious D being on HBO, but this was a new experience. And I definitely felt the heat of the pressure like, 'Oh fuck.'"[16]

> And I would go back to my hotel room after shooting and I would be frustrated that I had not gone as far as I could have or something. And I remember in the shower saying—this is embarrassing to admit—but I would chant, "ALL OF THE FUCKING WAYYY. ALL OF THE FUCKING WAYYY" like a fucking lunatic in the shower. Singing and screaming at myself in anger that I need to go all of the fucking way, because I'm only going half way.[17]

His tribal-like chanting worked wonders. Jack Black indeed went all of the fucking way.

In addition to getting Jack to do the film, the other challenge became who would we be able to find to keep up with him on-screen to play the third record store employee, Dick.

Dick might not be as aggressive as Barry is, but Dick's knowledge of music history—and his passion for finding the rarest of gems that you've never even heard of—reminds us of so many people we've all encountered in record stores. While Barry will try to guilt you into buying a record, Dick will use his knowledge to inform you of why you should have that record.

David Arquette came close to getting the part, and again, Hoffman's name was floated as was Troy Garrety's. Steve Zahn came in to audition, but according to Frears, Cusack felt Zahn was too much of a "surfer-type dude." Since there are no surfers in Chicago, that took Zahn out of the running.

Who did wind up getting the part was Hoffman's former roommate and longtime friend and collaborator, Todd Louiso.

At the time he was cast, Todd Louiso had a series of smaller roles under his belt in films like *Scent of a Woman*; *Stella*; *Billy Bathgate*; *Apollo 13*; and *The Rock*. In 1997 he got a more prominent role as he costarred with Joe Pesci and David Spade in *8 Heads in a Duffelbag*. But it was his scene-stealing role as Chad the Nanny in *Jerry Maguire* that really started to garner him some attention. One person who took notice of that performance was D.V. DeVincentis.

DeVincentis recalls,

> I loved Todd because of what he did in *Jerry Maguire*. I looked at that performance and I wasn't necessarily thinking that the role of Dick could be a repeat of that sort of performance or that kind of approach, but what I saw in the way he worked in *Jerry Maguire* was that he was going to bring something really interesting with that role of Dick.[18]

With a character like Barry that is inarguably larger-than-life every moment he graces the screen, you need a character like Dick to balance it all out. It's a performance that could only be portrayed by someone who understands on a deep level who this character is beyond the meek persona you see on the screen. Not only does he ground the film with his hilarious subtlety, he is also undeterred. No matter how many times Barry tries to shut him down, Dick never gives him any satisfaction. Despite their constant brother-like bickering, there's actually an incredibly solid relationship between Barry and Dick at the root of it all.

"The thing about Todd that I loved so much in *High Fidelity* is that he is Jack Black's perfect opposite number, and I think that would've been hard for any other actor," says Pink.

> We got really lucky with Todd. Todd was almost like this Ying to Jack's Yang in a way that had so much authority. Jack could pick on Todd all he wanted, and Todd was kind of an unmovable force of heart. He was kind of this force of serenity. He had this genuine heart that could not be diminished by Jack's insanity.[19]

"The three of them really formed an ensemble in a kind of way that you often have in the theater but often folks don't have onscreen," adds Simmons of their chemistry on-screen. "And I think maybe that's one of the reasons why so many people can see themselves in the story itself. Because those characters are so real."[20]

That chemistry that you see on-screen between Jack and Todd also managed to extend off camera. The two formed a bond while making the film. They would wind up hanging out after wrapping up for the day and—thanks to the ever-present Dan Koretzky—they would hit up local clubs and see bands such as Pavement.

At one point, they even wound up singing backup on a track for a Drag City artist. Sadly, neither Todd nor Jack can recall who the artist was or what the song was. Somewhere out there, though, there's a song that has background vocals featuring Jack Black and Todd Louiso.

"That was cool to be in close proximity to that kind of culture," Black recalls about his many nights spent in Chicago.

> And that was key to the success of the movie, too. I feel like it came at a time out of the indie rock steam of the '90s, because it came out in 2000 when it was still riding that crest of fascination with indie rock and indie small record stores. It's kind of the Last of the Mohicans. It's this last shining moment and we kind of captured it.[21]

There were countless parties throughout production, and Tenacious D even wound up doing a show at the House of Blues that many members of the *High Fidelity* cast and crew attended.

"Me and Cusack and D.V. and Steve went to see him," McGarvey recalls.

> It was the fucking best gig I had ever been to in my life. It was just incredible. Tenacious D, him and Kyle, played this gig where they had a monkey spunking all of the audience, spraying sperm all over the audience. It covered us all with this foam.[22]

Music taste, of course, comes into play heavily when you talk about *High Fidelity*, and especially when you talk about the characters of Barry and Dick. These are two characters who listen to music all day at work then go home and listen to more music. They are constantly defending their own tastes, making recommendations, and in the case of Barry, shitting all over the tastes of others that he feels are beneath him. Don't even *think* about asking Barry if they carry "I Just Called to Say I Love You."

So when it came to the actors, you had to find people who would fit into that world pretty naturally. Thankfully, the film lucked out when they cast Jack Black and Todd Louiso.

While *Tenacious D* and Black himself had an underground following back in 2000 when *High Fidelity* came out, the band has since found its rightful place in pop culture. His music career is just as synonymous with Jack Black as acting is at this point. To think, Jack Black has his eclectic taste in music thanks to some total stranger he met in a record store when he was a teenager in the 1980s.

At summer camp, all the cool kids were listening to Styx, specifically "Renegade." Another popular tune while Black was a kid was Journey's "Don't Stop Believin'." He was a fan of the whole *Escape* album, actually—so much so that he wound up going to the local record store to see what other Journey albums he could find.

"There was a dude that saw I was looking in the Journey section," says Black.

> And he looked over and was like, "Nah, dude." And he was just like such a cool, tall dude. You could just tell he was a badass. It was like a moment in an old western where he was like the Clint Eastwood of fucking heavy metal. He was like, "This is what you want over here. This is the record you need." And he handed me *Ozzy Osborne: Blizzard of Oz*. And I was like, "Oh! You are my leader. I will trust you!" And I put away the other fucking Journey album. He opened my world. He changed my life and opened the fucking portal to the dark side.[23]

As for Todd Louiso, he found it pretty easy to tap into Dick's Midwestern taste. This is because Louiso is a Midwesterner himself having been born and raised in Cincinnati, Ohio. Louiso also has a pretty varied taste in all different types of music and had his own record store experiences that he brought to the film.

"There used to be a store—like the store in the film—up in Hollywood," says Louiso. "And I went there a few times and just hung out and rooted around. It was on Highland, just north of Hollywood

Boulevard. It was exactly like in the film. The film was exactly like this place."[24]

In *High Fidelity*, there is this whole obsession with the top five. In the story, it serves as a way for the characters to pass the time. This is the type of world these guys live in. A world where everything you like can be boiled down to just five things. You can't go over. It has to be five.

The discussions are rooted deeply in the type of conversations you'd also have with your own friends. How many times do you recall sitting around, with nothing better to talk about, and wasting all matter of hours debating which artist sucks and which artist is underrated? It's something we all can relate to.

As a viewer, these top five lists are also a pretty genius way for you to get a deeper understanding of the character without it being too entangled within the story. A top five list of songs about death or musical crimes committed by Stevie Wonder in the 1980s will tell you exactly who these characters are without your feeling like the story is drowning in never-ending amounts of exposition.

Naturally, when you're talking about top five lists, the question has to be asked. What would be in Jack Black and Todd Louiso's top five albums of all time?

This question troubled both of them. When asked on the spot, Jack Black rattled off a list that was pretty solid. But still unsatisfied, he updated the list about a week later. "I wanna go all double albums," said Black during the follow-up call. "All the way across the board, to get maximum bang for the buck."[25]

His top five are

1. Led Zeppelin: *Physical Graffiti*
2. Rolling Stone: *Exile on Main St.*
3. The Beatles: *The White Album*

4. The Who: *Tommy*
5. Pink Floyd: *The Wall*[26]

Being the generous guy that he is, Black also came up with a bonus top five. His top five NBA players of all time. This is undisputable. It's not even really up for debate.

1. Michael Jordan
2. LeBron James
3. Magic Johnson
4. Larry Bird
5. Shaquille O'Neil[27]

When Todd was asked about his top five, he decided he couldn't quite narrow it down to just five. Instead, we got sixteen choices, including some where he couldn't narrow it down to a single album for a band. So those bands got the blanket any-album-by treatment. Hey, nobody said top fives were easy!

1. Prince: *1999*
2. Any Radiohead album
3. Beyoncé: *Lemonade*
4. Morphine: *Cure for Pain*
5. Beastie Boys: *Paul's Boutique*
6. Soul Coughing: *Ruby Vroom*
7. Big Audio Dynamite: *This Is Big Audio Dynamite*
8. Jane's Addiction: *Nothing's Shocking*
9. Khruangbin: *Con Todo el Mundo*
10. Midnight Star: *No Parking on the Dance Floor*
11. Eric B. and Rakim: *Follow the Leader*
12. Courtney Barnett: *A Sea of Split Peas*
13. Electric President: *S/T*

14. The Flaming Lips: *At War with the Mystics*
15. REM: *Murmur*
16. Any Joan As Police Woman album[28]

Narrowing down your five favorite records seems a lot easier in theory, doesn't it?

6

Assembling the Cast

With Rob, Dick, and Barry locked in, next up was the task of filling out the rest of the cast. While the three music obsessives take up a large chunk of the movie, it was casting everyone else—particularly Laura and Marie—that actually proved to be the most challenging. That's because the film wasn't filled with your standard girlfriend-archetype characters that romantic comedies have traditionally been obsessed with, particularly during that the era.

The girlfriends—both Laura and the ones of the past—were incredibly strong-willed, and had to be able to go toe-to-toe with Rob, while never losing their likability. Yes, they were frustrated with him. But they also had to possess the ability to stand their ground with him too. You had to buy that they would put up with someone like Rob, while also finding all of the redeeming qualities that lurk beneath the surface. There's a lot of different plates that had to be juggled with Laura. Therefore, you had to make sure you could find an actress who could handle it all and do so effortlessly.

This made Laura one of the toughest roles to cast in *High Fidelity*. While Stephen Frears could know instinctively just by looking at them that Todd Louiso and Jack Black were perfect for their respective parts, there were a number of hurdles he was facing with the character of Laura.

He first set out to find an American actress. Some of the actresses that they brought in to read included Halle Berry, Debra Messing,

Carla Gugino, Julianna Marguilies, Diane Lane, K. K. Dodds, Monica Potter, and Mary McCormack—who reportedly came close. Others who were at one time or another considered for the role included Joey Lauren Adams, Portia de Rossi, Maggie Gyllenhaal, Kim Gordon, and Sarah Jessica Parker.

"Stephen and I met with a number of women in New York," recalls DeVincentis. "Stephen and I sat down with Jennifer Lopez and had a long meeting. Stephen kicked me out of the meeting eventually because she and I were getting along too well. He's like, 'Out!' We were having a good time."[1]

However, Stephen was struggling to find someone who—as he puts it—didn't feel like she was old enough to be Rob's mother. DeVincentis wasn't quite sure what he meant by that or why. Eventually he came up with a theory that was confirmed by Frears.

Says DeVincentis,

> What I figured out was that it was somebody who has lived a life as an equal with Rob, but at a certain point, had pulled ahead of him and had become more adult. Whereas he sustained this world in which he didn't grow up. And so it had to be somebody who still was believable in putting up with this and having her foot in it. Being tired of it, but still understanding it. She's not somebody who was beyond it.[2]

In the midst of his search, Frears wound up in Germany, where he was attending the 1999 Berlin Film Festival. He was there with his film, *The Hi-Lo Country*. Frears recalls that while he was at the festival, all of the jurors were telling him to go and talk to this one actress in particular, a Danish actress named Iben Hjejle. "She's really good and she speaks English," they all told him. So he did, and after speaking with her, he had a gut instinct that she was right for the part.[3]

However, Iben Hjejle recalls that she was the one that had approached Stephen Frears first.

By this time, Hjejle was in her late-twenties and only had two films under her belt. She'd been born in Copenhagen, and her first on-screen acting job was in the 1996 film, *Portland*. Her second movie was a Dogme film, *Mifune's Last Song*. The film was a hit at the festival, having won the Silver Bear Grand Jury Prize, and Hjejle won an honorable mention for her performance. And the performance also got the attention of a certain Stephen Frears—or once again, it could've been vice versa, depending on whom you ask. Perhaps a combination of the two.

At the festival, Hjejle and a friend found themselves arguing over what the best Stephen Frears movie was. *Dangerous Liaisons* is what Hjejle said. *Gumshoe* is what her friend said. So they figured they'd go over and ask Stephen himself which was the better of the two.

"We walk up to him and we talk to him for about five minutes," Hjejle recalls. "Then Stephen turns to me and says, 'So you think you can act in an American accent?' I say, 'Absolutely, sir.' And I had no idea. He said, 'I think I have a part for you in my next film.'"[4]

After that meeting, Frears called Hjlejle and sent her the script and the book. She immediately loved both.

"Rob, is just the kind of boy that I had been falling in love with over and over again in my youth," she recalls. "So I kind of knew everyone in that script. Because the book takes place in Europe, it's also very recognizable to that Copenhagen music environment. So for me, there was absolutely no doubt."[5]

"Stephen works in a very intuitive way," Simmons adds. "So sometimes it's difficult for him to actually say specifically what it was that he wasn't seeing. I remember we saw quite a number of actresses. And he just felt when he met Iben that that's the one."[6]

After the Berlin Film Festival, Stephen Frears excitedly called the boys to tell them his big news that he'd finally found someone perfect to play Laura, and she was Danish. Of course their initial reaction of brief confusion was a natural reaction. Hjejle had only done two films, and neither of them in English. Would she really be up to such a big task? Laura is such an essential part of the entire film. Much like Rob, so much of the story rests on her shoulders.

Again, this was Stephen Frears we're talking about. He was a film-maker the three of them revered and still found themselves in dis-belief that they were working with him on only their second film as screenwriters. So they figured he must be onto something here and decided that they just had to trust him.

"We all trusted Stephen so implicitly," recalls DeVincentis. "He's incredible at casting and incredible at discovery. If you look at the people that had their first meaty role in a Stephen Frears movie, it's remarkable. It's fucking crazy all the people that he's introduced us to."[7]

At that point, it was decided that Frears, Cusack, and casting director Victoria Thomas would meet with Hjejle to do a chemis-try test. Because Hjejle had a son that was only a year old, she had requested that they travel to her. So the three all made the trip to Copenhagen so Iben and John could read together on camera.

That wound up sealing the deal. By the time they read together, it was clear to everyone in the room: she *had* to be Laura.

"She was a remarkable actress," Cusack said in an interview.

> I just knew she would be the perfect person because you need someone whose bullshit detector would look right through the idiocy of Rob, where she wouldn't have to say anything—like you just knew she already knew all of his moves, all of his tricks.[8]

The next step was making sure that her English would be up to par. To accomplish this, Hjejle worked with a dialect coach for three to five hours a day, making sure she got the accent just right.

Additionally, the filmmakers decided that they'd also give Laura a bit of a Danish background just to help balance things out.

"In that scene where she goes to the funeral, you can see they're all very Scandinavian," says Pink. "We had to kind of lean into the fact that she was an alt-punk rock girl. We embraced her nationality."[9]

With Laura cast, the next biggest challenge the film faced was Rob's other—albeit briefer—love interest, the musician Marie De Salle. Rob, Barry, and Dick first discover De Salle in a local nightclub. He winds up eventually having a one-night stand with LaSalle after she comes to visit Championship Vinyl.

It was important to everyone at first that they cast a real musician in the part. That's why they first set their sights on Liz Phair.

By this time, Liz Phair had already made a name for herself with the albums *Exile in Guyville*; *Whip-Smart*; and *Whitechocolatespaceegg*. She had been twice nominated in 1995 and 1996 for Grammy Awards in the category of Best Female Rock Vocals. She also happened to be a Chicagoan, who just so happened to know DeVincentis.

The two met in North Chicago and hit it off right away. They even wound up dating for a bit. When they first met, she was primarily a painter who recorded songs in her spare time. Eventually, the songs turned out to be game-changing, and she was off to the races. So by the time *High Fidelity* came around, DeVincentis was really pushing for her to get the part.

"We actually had a read through of the script in Chicago with Liz reading the role," DeVincentis recalls. "We did the reading at Joanie Cusack's house. And she was totally great. We're like, 'She's an actress. Oh my God!' But it wasn't right for the role."[10]

Frears had been wanting something—according to DeVincentis—"that seemed to be other-worldly in the world of that record store."

"We wanted her to be mystifying," adds Pink. "If it was Jewel or someone like that, that wouldn't be odd to a white dude in Chicago. So we wanted to find someone who could play it with this mysterious quality that he could be awed by who was also in the music world."[11]

Similarly to Laura, there was just nobody that seemed to be right for the part for Stephen. While they saw pretty much every actress in the 20- to 35-year-old range for Laura, they were looking for a musician when it came to Marie.

So some of the names that either came in to read or were at the very least considered included Mariah Carey, Sheryl Crowe, Gwen Stefani, Neneh Cherry, Lauryn Hill, Courtney Love, Lisa Stanfield, PJ Harvey, Victoria Adams, and even Aailyah.

Again, Stephen Frears just wasn't happy with anything that he was seeing. Then at one point, Lisa Bonet came in. Despite being known as an actress as opposed to a musician, she was just what Stephen had been looking for. It didn't hurt that Victoria Thomas and her went way back.

"I've known Lisa since she was actually in junior high school," Thomas recalls. "I was casting a student film at UCLA, and she came in to play one of the parts. So I've known her for a really long time. And I remember going to the first *Cosby Show* taping and thinking *Oh, I think this is going to be good*."[12]

Hard to believe, but by the time *High Fidelity* came out, it had already been fifteen years since she was first introduced to the world as one of "America's TV daughters" on the then-cultural touchstone that was *The Cosby Show*. She wound up getting spun off into her own show, *A Different World*, that showed her character Denise going off to college. After announcing her real life pregnancy, however, she left the show. Eventually, she went back to *The Cosby Show* but was fired in 1991 for creative differences. The tension between her and Cosby became tabloid fodder at the time.

After *The Cosby Show*, she did a small handful of roles in movies including *Bank Robber*; *Final Combination*; and *Enemy of the State*, which coincidentally was also cast by Thomas. When he cast her in the film, Frears was not even aware of her *Cosby Show* years, he says. She was cast solely because she was right for the part.

"She was so interesting and her own creature," says DeVincentis. "It really was like an alien landing in that record store."[13]

"There's not one redeeming character," Bonet said in an interview of the characters in the film with a laugh. "These men are pigs! I only got halfway through and then I realized that he kind of comes to his senses. He has a little bit of a meltdown, and we see some hope at the end."[14]

This only makes up one-fifth of Rob's top five worst breakups of all time. De Salle, of course, was never on that list. Ex number one is Alison Ashmore, played by Shannon Stillo. She is only seen in flashbacks as their fling happened for a fleeting moment back in junior high. One day, young Rob, played by Drake Bell, catches her making out with Kevin Bannister.

Ex number two is Penny Hardwick. She is every guy's dream girl in high school. Yet she isn't quite ready to go all the way. This manages to frustrate Rob, who is only interested in one thing at that point. So he breaks up with her and later discovers that she wound up sleeping with the guy she dated right after him. This causes him to ask the question no guy ever actually wants to hear the answer to: "Why not me?"

Some of the other names considered for Penny—that never actually came in to read for the part—were Cameron Diaz and Kristen Johnson. The part ended up going to Joelle Carter. Before *High Fidelity*, Carter had smaller parts in the films *The Horse Whisperer*; *Just One Time*; and *Suits*.

Ex number three is the one who seemingly did the most damage to Rob before Laura. This was Charlie, the eccentric, artistic type who seemed to be light-years out of Rob's league. In the film, we see him falling apart when he discovers that Charlie has left him for another guy named Marco. For Charlie they considered Nicole Kidman, Uma Thruman, and Charlize Theron before landing on Catherine Zeta-Jones.

DeVincentis wasn't sure if someone as glamorous as CZJ could play a "monster" like Charlie. Charlie had to be a lot rougher around the edges and really go out of her way to play mind games with Rob. Once she got on the set, however, the fear was alleviated. Obviously, she nailed the part and gave a pretty incredible performance.

"Catherine Zeta-Jones showed up on set," recalls Higgins, "and I don't think [she and Frears] had really met. And she got in that morning. We were in Wicker Park, and there was a look on his face like *My God, is she beautiful.* He looked at me with this grin, like only Stephen Frears could do."[15]

The last ex is Sarah Kendrew. Sarah and Rob's flame started after they both swore off the drama that had been so associated with their previous relationships. Both of them had been unceremoniously discarded, and sought out something that was more safe in a relationship or not-a-relationship type of ordeal. Naturally, Rob winds up catching feelings, at which point Sarah decides to end it. For Sarah, Cusack reunited with his *Say Anything* costar Lili Taylor.

In the film, Rob is not the only one whose love life is examined. We also get a glimpse into Dick's love life. In the record store, Dick bonds with a woman named Annaugh Moss. Almost instantly they wind up dating. For this part, Stephen Frears cast Sara Gilbert, who was only a year removed from *Roseanne* at this point. But as with *The Cosby Show*, Frears had never seen it. Instead, he based his casting on a small little indie movie she had done. According to Gilbert, Frears wasn't even aware of what *Roseanne* was.

John Cusack in High Fidelity. AUTHOR'S COLLECTION

The interior of Championship Vinyl. AUTHOR'S COLLECTION

The outside of Championship Vinyl. AUTHOR'S COLLECTION

Todd Louiso and Jack Black in High Fidelity. Author's Collection

Iben Hjejle and John Cusack in High Fidelity. Author's Collection

Lisa Bonet in High Fidelity. Author's Collection

John Cusack and Jack Black in High Fidelity. TBM/
Alamy Stock Photo

Jack Black in High Fidelity. Maximum Film/Alamy
Stock Photo

Stephen Frears on the set of High Fidelity. RGR Collection/Alamy Stock Photo

John Cusack and editor Mick Audsley during the editing of High Fidelity.
Courtesy of Phoebe Grigor

Steve Pink, D.V. DeVincentis, and Seamus McGarvey.
COURTESY OF PHOEBE GRIGOR

Jack Black, Todd Louiso, John Cusack, and Lisa Bonet in
High Fidelity. RGR COLLECTION/ALAMY STOCK PHOTO

John Cusack and Joan Cusack in High Fidelity. RGR
COLLECTION/ALAMY STOCK PHOTO

John Cusack in High Fidelity. MOVIESTORE COLLECTION/ALAMY STOCK PHOTO

Zoe Kravitz in the Hulu series, High Fidelity. ALBUM/ALAMY STOCK PHOTO

Nick Hornby at the Edinburgh International Book Festival. JEREMY SUTTON-HIBBERT/ALAMY STOCK PHOTO

John Cusack in High Fidelity. TBM/ALAMY STOCK PHOTO

John Cusack, Jack Black, Todd Louiso, and Tim Robbins. AJ PICS/ALAMY STOCK PHOTO

John Cusack and Iben Hjejle in High Fidelity. Maximum Film/Alamy Stock Photo

Stephen Frears, Nick Hornby, and D.V. DeVincentis on the set of High Fidelity. RGR Collection/Alamy Stock Photo

"I have a memory of him apologizing that the role wasn't bigger," Gilbert remembers. "And I thought *What a kind man*. I'm just so thrilled to be invited to the party. Of course it's always nice to have a big part. But I was just happy to be there."[16]

"I just thought it was a good script," Gilbert adds. "It's relatable. I was so excited to work with Stephen Frears, and I liked the character because it was more innocent and wide-eyed and different from what I had done. I liked that departure."[17]

Of course, Rob also needed to have a personal foe, and he does. After Laura and Rob break up, she winds up seeing Ian, a ponytail-rocking, all-around douchebag. After he finds out about their love affair, Rob starts doing some investigating, and discovers that Ian actually lives in the apartment right above the one he shared with Laura.

For Ian, the role called for someone who could play it completely over-the-top in how comedically pompous he was. It had to be the perfect blend of charm, self-righteousness, and smarm. To play the role, they landed on bringing it all full circle with Tim Robbins.

Robbins, of course, is the reason they knew who Jack Black was. Cusack, DeVincentis, Pink, and Black had all treaded the boards, if you will, at Robbins's the Actor's Gang. Not only that, but Cusack had appeared in *Bob Roberts* and *The Cradle Will Rock*. So it was time for Robbins to return the favor, ponytail and all. Had Robbins not come in to play Ian, they had a list of possible names that included Jason Patric, Dylan McDermott, and even Kevin Bacon.

When Robbins was asked to appear in the film by Cusack, he had only one request.

"He asked me to do this part," Robbins said in an interview. "But I've got one request. I need a wig. Because I wanted to look like Steven Segal."[18]

In *High Fidelity*, the character of Liz serves as a go-between during the more-tense moments of Rob and Laura's breakup. A mutual friend of both, we find the character caught in the middle before she eventually confronts Rob and calls him a "fucking asshole" after she finds out that Rob cheated on Laura.

Having Joan Cusack play the role of Liz was a natural fit for a number of reasons. Of course, there is the fact that she and her brother John had acted alongside each other countless times before, as well as her having worked with Frears before in the film *Hero*.

But having Joan Cusack in the film was also a huge get for *High Fidelity*. Aside from just the work she had done with her brother, she was fresh off of her second Academy Award nomination for her role in the Kevin Kline comedy *In and Out*. It also didn't hurt having another born-and-raised Chicagoian in a movie that served as an absolute love letter to the city.

Next up was finding the two young actors to play Vince and Justin, the two characters the film's screenwriters added to the script to give Rob a new purpose career-wise. To find these characters, they turned to local talent. When you're looking for young, up-and-coming local talent in Chicago to play quirky characters in a movie, look no further than Chicago's own the Second City.

Ben Carr and Chris Rehmann were both taking classes at Chicago's famed the Second City while the film was casting. Claire Simon, founder of Simon Casting, was handling local casting. Simon went in and saw both Carr and Rehmann, who were in separate classes. Both were asked to come in and audition for the film.

Of his audition, Carr recalls being shocked when he walked in the room and discovered that he'd be auditioning in front of Stephen Frears. *The Grifters* had been one of his favorite films. When it came time to audition, "all ability to try to act or speak or talk was gone," Carr says. Still, he impressed them enough that he was asked to come back in and improvise. Tim O'Malley, an instructor at the Second City, worked with both Carr and Rehmann and helped them prepare. To Carr's surprise, the call came in that they got the part.[19]

Part of Vince and Justin's role—they were dubbed by Barry as "those little skate fuckers"—was their distinctive looks. Rehmann had bleached blonde hair with leopard spots in it, while Carr had bleached his hair and then dyed it bright pink. This served as a controversial subject at his high school graduation, the high school being rather strict against Carr walking to accept his diploma while sporting pink hair. He eventually got it dyed to an acceptable shade so he could still graduate.

Finally, Natasha Gregson Wagner was cast in the role of Caroline Fortis. Caroline is the reporter who does an interview with Rob at the end of the film and serves as a temptation just as Rob has rekindled his relationship with Laura. The daughter of Natalie Wood and Richard Gregson, Wagner had been working steadily all throughout the 1990s. Her first film role was in 1992's *Fathers and Sons*. Following that, she appeared in *Buffy the Vampire Slayer*; *High School High*; *Two Girls and a Guy*; *Another Day in Paradise*; *Dogtown*; and the made-for-TV movie *Hart to Hart*: *Secrets of the Hart* alongside her stepfather Robert Wagner.

This was the only casting that DeVincentis wasn't actively involved in as he was back in Chicago at the time. Frears later called him up and told him about Wagner. "Cool," DeVincentis replied. "She's great, if you think she's right for it."[20]

So Wagner got the part. During the course of production, Wagner and DeVincentis wound up falling in love. They eventually married in 2003, though they ended up divorcing in 2008. Had Stephen Frears not requested that the boys restore Rob's last temptation from the book, Wagner never would have been cast in *High Fidelity*.

Oddly enough, there were a few different love stories mixed into the *High Fidelity* shoot. It seems sort of fitting, in a strange way. The other love connection that happened was with Steve Pink. Just by nature of being in the Midwest to shoot the film, he reconnected with an old college friend. They wound up dating, and are now married and still together to this day. This is something that Pink says would not have happened if he wasn't back in Illinois making *High Fidelity*.

"Definitely the movie was, I'm sure, in some part doing it to us," Pink says of the blossoming relationships. "Better than us making a serial killer movie. Then we'd all be in jail, if you follow that logic."[21]

Luckily, nobody wound up going to jail. Instead everyone was in Chicago in the spring and eager to get the cameras rolling on *High Fidelity*.

7

Shooting

Nearly four years after the book was first optioned in 1995, cameras were finally ready to roll on *High Fidelity* in Chicago. D.V. DeVincentis, Steve Pink, and John Cusack were getting to make the exact film they set out to make, which as anyone in the industry can attest to, is rarified air.

Even more, they were getting to make that movie in their old stomping ground in Wicker Park, far from the walls of the Hollywood home of DeVincentis where he first mapped out the Chicago storyline. While the critics would still have to wait another year before realizing the "Americanization of a British property" trope would hold no weight here, everyone involved knew exactly what they had.

The filming started on April 26, 1999. Ironically enough, the entire first day of filming would eventually hit the cutting room floor.

The first day featured a scene in which John Cusack as Rob gets a call from a woman with an insanely rare record collection. She has everything from *God Saves the Queen* to *My Baby* to *Only the Lonely*. When he arrives at her home, she reveals that it's her cheating husband's collection and she wants to unload the entire collection for only $50. Rob's morals wind up getting in the way, and he proclaims that he couldn't do that to a fellow collector. For all of Rob's flaws, he can still manage to empathize with a fellow die-hard music lover. The sale isn't made, except for one Otis Redding single.

The scene itself is very funny, and it was scripted pretty much exactly as Hornby had conceived it in his original novel. To boot, Beverly D'Angelo's performance in the scene was also terrific, proclaiming that her motive was to be "poisonous but fair." Everything about the scene itself works brilliantly. But after reviewing the final cut of the film, something about the scene didn't quite sit right with Stephen Frears.

"Stephen just thought it didn't work," DeVincentis remembers.

> And she was sort of doing us a favor by doing this. And he called her up and said, "Look, it's my fault. I didn't do it right. I feel like I know how to do it. Can you please come back so we can redo the scene?" And she said okay, because she's a total sport. So she comes back, we did it again, and then we cut the scene.[1]

Frears eventually realized why the scene didn't work. He said to D.V. that it wasn't the way he did it. The scene just didn't belong in the movie.

"I understand why it went," says Hornby. "It was a self-contained scene that doesn't really drive the story forward. And that's exactly the kind of stuff that you can afford to do in a novel that you can't do in a movie."[2]

Funny enough, day two saw production shoot a scene with Rob's dad, who was played by Harold Ramis. Ramis, of course, directed D'Angelo in the first *Vacation* film. They also have another thing in common. Both of their scenes were cut from *High Fidelity*.

"Years later, I sat down into my seat at the Chicago Theater for a Leonard Cohen concert," DeVincentis recalls. "And I heard behind me a whisper in my ear 'You motherfucker.' And I turned around and it was Harold. He was like, 'You cut me out. How could you cut me out?'"[3]

Nevertheless, the cameras rolled on. The April start date actually came out of something Frears had said. Frears recalled wanting to make sure they did the film between the infamous Chicago cold and heat. So they started production in late April and wrapped by the Fourth of July.

McGarvey had a very specific look that he wanted to capture for *High Fidelity*. For the first scene they shot where Rob speaks directly to the camera, McGarvey wanted to track in on a wide-angle lens. As for lighting, he wanted it to be extremely colorful and contrasty. As he describes it, he was looking for almost a "poppy feel." After all, given the world that this film was set in, it would make total sense for the film to have a more experimental, alt-like vibe to it. Since McGarvey had spent a lot of time working on music videos, it was a pretty natural fit it seemed like. The goal was to shoot it like the type of film that Rob, Barry, and Dick would actually be impressed by and relate to.

When Frears saw the first bit of rushes, however, it became clear that he didn't share the same vision that McGarvey had. In fact, he flat out hated what he saw.

McGarvey recalls,

> He was like, "Stop ruining my film with your fucking photography. Just photograph the actors, stick the actors there, and let the actors do their thing. Stop putting photography all over my film."[4]

Since he was worried by this point that he could be fired, McGarvey agreed to tone it down. From there on, the film was stylized more conventionally, with McGarvey still managing to add his flourishes throughout.

McGarvey continues,

> His films are about the human condition and beautifully told silently and honestly. And he was absolutely right. It's just that I

was a young buck cinematographer wanting to make my mark
with something fancy and startling, as a lot of people do. But
Frears was so right, and he taught me about restraint.[5]

"Seamus brought an energy to the visual approach of the film
that always had energy, but it also was very laid-back," says Pink. "It
wasn't so intentional that it was distracting. So he had this ability to
put a lot of energy into the frames he chose. The way he approached
scenes was amazing and it taught me a ton."[6]

When everyone thinks about their favorite *High Fidelity* scenes,
it all comes back to the record store. Production didn't start filming
in the store until day eleven, which was the beginning of the third
week. It sort of makes sense when you think about just how crucial
these scenes are. It was best to wait until everyone more or less found
their rhythm.

The topics of discussion in the store are pretty much exactly
what you'd hear in a record store. The passioned arguments, the
listing, the not-so-quietly judging someone's musical tastes before
the door even has a chance to fully close. Anyone who has spent
any time in a retail environment knows just how integral these conversations are just to make the day go by faster. While the topics of
discussion may seem banal or of little importance to someone else,
to the employees, those pointless diversions from doing productive
work are crucial.

The scenes themselves are just as authentic as the store's aesthetic. While there's magic sprinkled throughout the entire movie,
there's something about those scenes in the record store that just
brings the movie even more to life. Much of that is the result of
the terrific chemistry John Cusack, Jack Black, and Todd Louiso
had. Louiso and Black's pseudo-antagonistic attitude particularly
makes for some of the most memorable scenes in the movie.

"I remember an executive saying to me, 'Do you need all those scenes in the store,'" recalls Frears. "I said, 'Are you out of your fucking mind? They're absolutely gold dust.'"[7]

The record store gives us two of the arguably best sequences in the movie. First is the introduction of Dick and Barry. The first time we see Dick, he is actually waiting outside for Rob to get there. But Barry's entrance is a bit more intense.

Black recalls,

> When we were going to shoot it, I was like, "Oh fuck. This is a big one. I've got to do something!! There's got to be fireworks here." So I just kind of went at it. There's a little bit of fight or flight response when you're in that kind of situation, where it feels like you're acting for your life. Like you'll die if you don't fucking get a response. So I kind of went crazy.[8]

As Barry enters the store, he is humming a riff from *Jacob's Ladder* by Rush. At the time it didn't occur to Steve Pink that they'd need to secure the rights to the song just to have Jack Black humming it.

"I remember being deep in post," says Pink, "and Kathy Nelson being like, 'Hey. You know we've got to pay Rush to use "Jacob's Ladder"?' We never asked him to change the solo. It just never occurred to me that we needed to get the rights to that."[9]

Jack Black going crazy, in his own words, became the norm when he was on-screen—so much so that Seamus McGarvey had to adapt to how he shot Barry's scenes.

"It was like wildlife photography," McGarvey says.

> Because his choreography of action would sort of dart around. So you couldn't set up a shot with him. He was so kind of alive as an actor, that you basically had to set the camera in a position

and light it. It could go in any direction he felt it was going to go, and he did.[10]

"I remember the first shot Jack did," Frears remembers. "Then I tried to move in for a closeup and I realized he was hopeless. He could only be himself. So then I thought, *Well, I'll put two cameras on him.*"

"They would show the rushes at lunchtime," Frears continues. "And then once word got out about Jack, people would come from all over the studio to see his rushes."[11]

The other moment in the record store that everybody seems to want to talk about is the epic fight scene between Rob, Dick, Barry, and Laura's new beau, Ian. The fight scene itself is comedically over-the-top, which you can get away with because it's all done in fantasy sequence. The button is the moment when Dick pulls the air conditioner vent out of the wall and, very uncharacteristically, crushes Ian with it. When it came time to shoot the scene, Stephen Frears knew exactly how he wanted it shot. It had to be a western.

However, the tag to the scene almost didn't happen because there was an issue with the air conditioner when the time came to shoot the scene. They were running behind schedule and it almost wasn't included, but John Cusack and D.V. DeVincentis were adamant, according to Todd Louiso. The air conditioner had to stay. With only a few takes and a ticking clock, they managed to have it all come together in the zero hour.

The shot didn't completely go off without injury, however. No, none of the actors got injured during the fight. It was actually McGarvey who got injured. He was on the floor with the camera angled up toward the air conditioner as it was coming down.

"We had such fun," recalls McGarvey, "to the extent that it kind of got a little bit out of hand. I got hit by the air conditioner. We did that final shot that ends the sequence where the air conditioner comes down on his head, and it came down on mine. It actually drew blood."[12]

As for the record store itself, the set was stacked wall-to-wall with what can only be described as heaven for any music obsessive. All the painstaking details, as well as charts constructed by DeVincentis, paid off. The end result was perhaps the greatest, most authentic fake record store that had ever been committed to film.

Higgins says of the set,

> Me being a music junkie, I had my eye on all those albums when we bought them. Originally they had spanned a lot of those shelves with vinyl. After a week or two, they started to overload. They had to over the weekend take the vinyls out of the covers and dispose of them. And it just broke my heart because some of those albums were really great.[13]

When it came to the on-screen chemistry between the three characters, it was pretty organic. John Cusack and Jack Black had, of course, known each other for years via the Actor's Gang but this was Todd Louiso's introduction into the fray. Thankfully, the group hit it off pretty fast, especially Jack and Todd.

While Jack Black may have gone on to become the breakout star of the film, that is not to diminish what John Cusack brought to the film as Rob. On the contrary. While he does need to be surrounded by a strong ensemble in order for the film to work as a whole, so much of it all rests on his shoulders.

That all comes back to the choice of having Rob speak directly to the camera. We, as an audience, are witnessing every internal thought that a character can have even down to all the different scenarios he wishes would play out in crucial moments, such as an ex-girlfriend's current beau confronting him at work. If this happened to any of us, we no doubt would have three similar ways to handle the situation play out in our own head in real time.

Cusack adapted to the challenges that came with playing Rob with a natural ease that is seldom seen. His *Cusackian* charm that cinemagoers have come to recognize—with his endearing half-smile and wide-eyed facial expressions and giving off the confidence of being the coolest guy in the room even when he isn't—is on full display here.

Yes, at a certain point, John Cusack has even become his own category, with his performances being described as *Cusackian* for their *Cusackness*. As for what either of these words means, John Cusack isn't too entirely sure. Cusack told the *New York Times* he didn't know what *Cusackness* means, the term having been coined by Cusack's *Say Anything* costar John Mahoney.

> Probably that was the first movie I did where I got to create a lot more than was in the text. When I got offered *Say Anything*, I didn't really want to do it. I felt that Lloyd didn't have enough of a worldview. So I put a lot of my own sensibility into it. Maybe that's what John meant.[14]

Naturally, *High Fidelity* gave Cusack a lot of room to add his own sensibilities into the mix given his contribution as not just the star of the film, but also as a cowriter and producer. If you had to write an essay in college about *Cusackness*, basing your definition on John Cusack's definition of the term, *High Fidelity* would have to be at the forefront. *High Fidelity* has Cusack's charisma on full display.

In addition to his strengths as an actor on-screen, Cusack was just as generous with his fellow actors off-screen. He was gracious in regard to his interactions with his fellow actors and managed to help them give even better performances as a result just by how he'd engage with them in off-camera acting.

"He's so good at it," DeVincentis says of his off-camera delivery.

> I never understood that it was a skill until I watched John do
> it. Because when you're off camera for another actor, you give
> them what they need to get where they need to go. It sounds
> very obvious, but it isn't always the same performance you give
> when you're on camera. Sometimes you need to be more subtle
> or sometimes you need to be bigger. But whatever it is, you need
> to be completely focused on giving them what they need. And
> John is incredible at doing that.[15]

It was this off-camera delivery that helped bring the best out of
perhaps the film's most famous cameo. More on that later . . .

"I think a lot of people can relate to him," Lisa Bonet said in an
interview about working with John Cusack. "Men can relate to him.
Women can relate to him, in terms of seeing themselves with him.
Men putting themselves in his position."[16]

Frears noted a big shift when it came to working with Cusack this
time around, as opposed to the experience he had with him on *The
Grifters*. "John was sort of grown up," says Frears.

> When I did *The Grifters*, he'd be very good for about two hours
> a day. And then you'd eventually arrange that day's shooting
> around those two good hours. By the time we did *High Fidel-
> ity*, he was able to take responsibility for the whole film. So he'd
> grown up. He'd become much more adult. He was very well
> cast.[17]

Ask any member of the cast or crew, and everyone seems to look
back on that time fondly. As anyone who has worked on a film knows,
typically you'll remember the negative experiences more than than
the positive ones. In the case of *High Fidelity*, everyone generally has
nothing but fond recollections of making the film.

"I don't really remember it being that difficult," recalls Rudd Simmons. "We didn't have stunts or car chases or visual effects. It was kind of just the thing that Stephen does so well. It's about characters and his actors that are in a room talking."[18]

Of course with any production, hiccups occur throughout. Every production—no matter how much talent you have behind it—is going to face its own challenges on a fairly regular basis. It's even more difficult when you are on location and far away from the studio. *High Fidelity* was no exception.

"We were in the rain a lot," says unit production manager Billy Higgins. "It's one thing to have a rain scene out in front of an apartment, but he would do blocks of rain, which is really a hard setup."[19]

One day, DeVincentis and Pink showed up on set only to find that production was behind schedule as a result of the rain machine breaking down. Frustrated, DeVincentis went up to Frears and asked why they had to shoot the scene in the rain anyway. Frears fired back, "Because you fucking wrote it that way!"[20]

Thankfully, the rain machine was eventually fixed, and production rolled on. To be fair, the copious amounts of rain in the film actually add something to every scene. Whenever we see Rob at his lowest—whether he's just discovered that his girlfriend Charlie has cheated on him or he's just left Laura's dad's funeral and is waiting for the bus—the image of him in the pouring rain adds another layer of vulnerability to the character.

It's the old idea of *How can this day get any worse?* that every single one of us can relate to. It makes Rob seem even more pathetic in those moments and further humanizes him for the audience. As we see a man standing there with defeat dripping off him, it makes him that much easier to sympathize with, despite his various shortcomings and flaws.

When you make a movie, it's common to have the screenwriters on set, but it's not always a given. It's especially not always a given that the writers will be on set every single day. Obviously, John Cusack would be on set, but so were DeVincentis and Pink, who were also producers on the film. Frears typically asks that the writers be on set when he makes a movie. This allows him to change a line or a scene on a whim. It's definitely an advantage having the writers very involved in the entire filming process.

So if there was more that had to be done with a particular scene, the trio would either go into Cusack's trailer or the trailer that DeVincentis and Pink shared and get to work. As anyone who works in the industry knows, there's always work on a script that can be done even when you're in the midst of a hectic production schedule.

"The worst thing that can happen with Stephen is if he arrives on set and he runs through it and he looks around and says, 'Well I don't know what I'm shooting,'" DeVincentis says.

> We learned that if he says that, you're fucked. If he doesn't feel like he knows what he's shooting, he's not going to be like, "Oh, we'll just shoot it and figure it out later." Stephen has to know. He has to have authority about what it is. It has to make sense to him. If there's a problem, you have to figure it out and you have to correct it.[21]

There were two occasions during filming where production was delayed while the trio figured out why the scene wasn't working or how it could be made better. In the end, the scenes wound up coming together in the best way possible. According to DeVincentis, these disruptions actually made the film better.

"This was one of the most important things anyone has ever said to me as a filmmaker ever," Pink recalls. "We were in the trailer and we were under the gun and we had to write something. And Frears said, 'There's no time to be inspired. Just get it right.'"[22]

Ask anyone who has ever worked on a Stephen Frears story, and they will tell you all sorts of wonderful, quirky, eccentric, and endearing tales of the filmmaking legend at work. Frears is direct and knows exactly what he wants, down to the tiniest detail. To watch him work is to watch a true cinematic master, making magic happen right before your very eyes.

Incidentally, he manages to do this while standing back and letting the actors do their thing. Some directors have a very micromanaging style when it comes to making a film. That is not the Stephen Frears way. He puts all of his faith and trust in the actors he works with. If he isn't quite getting what he wants, his direction is simple. "Do it better," he will say. Nothing less and nothing more.

Is it super direct? Yes. But it is never meant as belittling or insulting. It's all there in the words. He knows the actor can give a better performance than what he is seeing. That is what he is conveying with those three words. He's not being overly critical. Instead, he is just telling the actor they need to do it better.

"It underlines how Stephen looks at actors," says DeVincentis. "To him they are, they have mystical powers and he is continually in awe of them. And you can see it when you watch him watch them work."[23]

"I always felt like, 'I don't know if he likes me. He's never saying anything nice to me,'" Jack Black recalls. "But later he told me he loved me and he loved what I was doing. And he's like, 'If I don't say anything negative, that means that I love it.'"[24]

Sara Gilbert had the same experience. "I'd go up to him and say, 'So here's what I'm doing. There are a couple options. Would you like me to do more of this? Or would you prefer I do more of that?' And he would just look at me and say, 'I trust you.'"[25]

"Frears taught me pretty much everything I know about directing, because I used to go and basically try to interview him between

camera blocking and lighting," says Pink. "During lighting, sometimes there'd be a lot of time, and I'd just go and ask Stephen questions about directing."[26]

While Cusack, DeVincentis, and Pink were all producers on the
film, Frears wound up turning to Pink a lot more than Cusack and
DeVincentis when he needed a producer's input. Naturally Pink—
who eventually went on to become an accomplished director—
excelled in those moments.

"Steve is like an extraordinary producer," says DeVincentis.
"Knowing what I know now about producers, if I were to go back
and look at the fifteen-year-old Steve Pink, I'd be like, 'That guy's
going to be a great producer, as well as a writer and director.'"[27]

As much as Frears had a more hands-off approach with the
actors, he of course always maintained full control of the set. That
is sort of his charm. He will interject when he needs to and tell you
to do it better. But the best thing he feels he can do for an actor is let
them find their own way. DeVincentis notes that he has never seen a
director who does a better job of talking to actors and putting them
at ease than Stephen Frears.

When he was frustrated or wasn't seeing the film he had in his
head, you would know it. Jack Black recalls a particular instance
where he looked over at Stephen Frears lying on the floor of the
record store set and saying, to nobody in particular, "I'm too old to
direct this film."[28]

"He got really upset about something I can't remember, planning
wise," says Hjejle.

> And then he said, "I'm leaving! That's enough for today." He
> took me with him so they couldn't shoot anymore. And then he
> took me by the hand and put me into the van and he told the
> driver, "Just take me away from here. Just go the hell anywhere."
> So we drove around for a bit and sat and talked. And he said,

"Okay, we're going to go to the most expensive restaurant we can find, and we'll have dinner on somebody's expense."[29]

Another staple Stephen Frears story from production is the time that Frears and McGarvey almost met their maker en route to set one day. McGarvey was staying not too far from Frears, so he would drive Frears to set every morning. One particular morning, McGarvey was hungover after partying the night before, so Frears agreed to drive instead.

> We drove onto the freeway, but he drove the wrong way on the freeway. He drove up the off ramp. And we were suddenly on the fucking freeway, with juggernauts coming right at us. And we drove over to the side, and the police arrived immediately. They were like, *What the hell?* Frears rolled down the window and went, "I'm terribly sorry. I'm English."[30]

By the time you see the finished product of a Stephen Frears movie, you can see that his straight-to-the-point approach works. The performances he gets are real, authentic, and also have a raw and rough-around-the-edges feel to them.

Stephen also knows how to handle the sex scene in a film delicately. As anyone with a knowledge of sex scenes knows, there're all sorts of standards and protocols in place to ensure both safety and comfortability for the performers. There's a lot of fragility that you have to be mindful of when it comes to carefully constructing the scene through blocking.

The sex scene in *High Fidelity* that takes place between Laura and Ian, however, is supposed to be performed in an over-the-top fashion. Much like the fight scene, it's all taking place in Rob's head. So frankly, the more ridiculous and far-fetched, the better the end result would be in this instance. All realism can go out the window, replaced by sheer erotic camp, as Rob proclaims, "No woman in the history of the world is having better sex than the sex you are having with Ian . . . in my head."

Still, Stephen Frears decided to go above and beyond to make sure that his performers, particularly Iben, were as comfortable as possible. He wound up stepping to the side and letting women from the hair and makeup department direct the scene in his place. This made for a scene that Hjejle describes as "the only fun sex scene I've been a part of."

Recalls Hjejle,

> Stephen sat there and he called over the walkie and he said, "Can I please have all of the women on set?" It was only me and Tim Robbins, Stephen Frears, the cinematographer, and maybe five or eight ladies from the makeup and costume department. And he said, "You're going to make this the steamiest, sexiest, funniest sex scene we've ever seen." And so they did. They said, "Try and walk your fingers over Iben's bum. And try and do that and try and do that. Do a Tarzan attitude." And Stephen mainly sat and held his eyes in the corner.[31]

"I remember thinking, 'Oh this is rather good,'" Frears recalls about watching the sex scene once they were done with it. "'It's very unexpected. This isn't what I would've done.' It wasn't my idea to do it the way they did it. It was very, very striking."[32]

Over the course of making a movie, it is not uncommon for everyone to become a tight-knit group. When you've got a movie like *High Fidelity*, however, the reality is that many members of the cast and crew already know each other. Frears had brought Tim Bevan, Rudd Simmons, and editor Mick Audsley with him to the film. Cusack, DeVincentis, and Pink, of course, were already a tight group. With them came their friends Jack Black and Tim Robbins; Cusack's *Say*

Anything costar Lili Taylor; Cusack's sister Joan; and even his father Dick, who played the priest who presides over Laura's dad's funeral service.

You really get the sense that the shoot was a family affair. Because of this, a lot of the getting-to-know-each-other in the first few weeks wasn't needed. From the offset, it felt like the dynamic was exactly where it should be.

So while some people involved in the shoot describe the shoot as being tough or difficult (while also not being able to recall many specifics of why this was), the overall sense you get is just how much everyone got along at the end of the day. *High Fidelity* indeed forged a family—even beyond those who knew each other going into the project—and one whose paths would continue to cross for years and years to come.

"It was really one of the only times when I was like, *I don't know if this is going to be interesting to anybody else, but it's damn interesting to me.*" Pink recalls about the experience of making the film. "How you wrestle with your relationships that you've fucked up, in a city that you love, and you're trying to figure out how to get your head out of your ass and become a decent person, I was trying to do that."[33]

Production on *High Fidelity* wrapped on July 2, 1999. The very next day, McGarvey married his then-girlfriend Phoebe on Chicago's Damon L platform. The entire cast and crew were on hand for the big day. His best man was Stephen Frears.

"Cusack rented a boat," recalls McGarvey.

> Me and Phoebe went out on this boat and went out on the lake. And there was the biggest fireworks display that there's ever been in Chicago for the Fourth of July. The last Fourth of July of the millennium. I'll never forget that as long as I live.[34]

High Fidelity had a revolving door of talented actors and actresses coming in and going out throughout. The likes of Lisa Bonet, Tim Robbins, Catherine Zeta-Jones, and more make incredibly memorable appearances throughout. But no matter how good they are, there is only one Bruce Springsteen . . .

8

The Boss

On any set, be it film, television, commercial, music video, or otherwise, the director is the boss. He is the one who's overseeing everything and has a crew of people making sure that what he is seeing play out in front of him is true to the vision he has in his head. His boss will be the studio, or if it's an independent film made without a studio, whoever is putting up the money. The bigger the director is, however, the more the studio's feedback becomes just light suggestions that the director can find unique or clever ways to circumvent.

On *High Fidelity*, Stephen Frears was the film's boss. As mentioned, he had a knack for being hands-off while remaining firmly in control 100 percent of the time. Then of course, there was the other boss. Rather, there was the day that the Boss came to shoot a scene for the film. *High Fidelity* surely has a stellar cast and a revolving door of great cameos. But when you think of the ultimate cameo in *High Fidelity*, well, there is only one. Bruce Springsteen.

The idea of having Bruce Springsteen be the voice inside Rob's head was thrown out during the writing process. This was because Springsteen is a constant thread that exists in Hornby's novel. In the book, at one point Rob even wonders, "What would Springsteen do?" The film took this concept and ran with it.

However, it wasn't present in all of the earliest versions of the script. In the draft that was worked on with Frears in London, for instance, Springsteen acting as the voice in Rob's head was nowhere to be found. Instead, Rob starts comparing his life to a Bruce Springsteen song in a fashion that's not unlike how it is in the book.

"There's this Springsteen song, 'Bobby Jean,' off *Born in the USA*," says Rob in the second draft of the script. "About a girl who's left town years before and he's pissed off because he didn't know about it, and he wanted to say goodbye, tell her that he missed her, and wish her good luck. Well, I'd like my life to be like a Springsteen song. Just once."[1]

Rob sums this all up with a motivational speech to himself, which is also very similar to the speech that would find itself in the finished film.

> I'd like to call up all those people and ask them how they are and whether they've forgiven me, and tell them that I have forgiven them. And say good luck, goodbye. No hard feelings. And then they'd feel good and I'd feel good. We'd all feel good. I'd feel clean, and calm, and ready to start again. That'd be good. Great even.[2]

In the final version of the script, he's a Yoda-like figure that helps set Rob on the path he needs to be on. While it's only about a minute, it is quite essential to the film. The script needed someone to be his internal consciousness and larger than life, someone who, even in his head, Rob would be in awe of. If it was a fictional person, they wouldn't have anywhere near the same impact. It had to be Bruce. It just had to be.

However, there were versions of the script between the second draft and the finalized version that didn't mention Springsteen at all. This, one imagines, would have to do with just what a big deal it'd be to have the Boss play along.

Getting someone of Springsteen's stature would be about as major a coup as one could dream up for a modestly budgeted romantic comedy set in a Chicago record store. He was more than just a legendary musician by this point. He seemed to exist on another plane entirely. Getting him to do a cameo in a movie is just one of those things that would normally seem out of the realm of possibility.

Think of it like this. By the time they shot the film in 1999, Bruce Springsteen had never acted on screen before, be it on television or in film. Sure, he had been on television more times than you could ever count via talk shows, interviews, concerts, news reels, and more. Clearly the last thing Bruce Springsteen needed was more exposure.

But he also had never acted in a narrative film or TV show. To this day, there have been only two times that Springsteen has been featured in a narrative feature film. A film named *Broken Poet* that came out in 2020, and *High Fidelity*.

Just how did they manage to score Bruce Springsteen? You would think that there would be some big, complicated story in which the end result just so happened to be securing Springsteen for the film. But in actuality, it was as simple as a phone call from John Cusack.

> When I was doing *Grosse Pointe Blank* or *High Fidelity*, you could have personal relationships with the musicians. You could just call them up. Like, for example, I got some Dylan songs, I screened the movie for Jeff Rosen, and Dylan gave us "Most of the Time" for *High Fidelity*. So between Kathy and I, we knew a lot of people in the music business, a lot of artists.
>
> I think the artists probably felt like we're giving their music a big showcase and not just needle dropping them in for some commercial catch up. So I just called Bruce and said, "Look, I know this is a weird question, but do you want to play yourself in a film talking to me in my head?" And he went, "Yeah!"[3]

During production, there were still some questions over whether or not Bruce Springsteen would actually commit. There was still a lot of back and forth. One thing was clear though. The mountain wasn't coming to Mohammed, so Mohammed had to go to the mountain.

After production wrapped in Chicago, word came back that Springsteen would meet with them in a recording studio in New York. So Frears, Cusack, DeVincentis, Pink, Seamus McGarvey, and Kathy Nelson all traveled to New York to film with Springsteen. Even on the day of the shoot, however, uncertainty was still in the air. Not unlike the famous lore of not knowing whether Bill Murray would show up on set or not, the question became *Is this actually going to happen?*

"It was the kind of thing," DeVincentis recalls. "I remember being there and going, 'This totally might not happen.' And then he showed up."[4]

When he did show up, everyone was sort of in awe. Everyone, that is, except for Frears. According to McGarvey, Frears "couldn't give a damn about the iconic nature of Springsteen." To Frears, the Boss was just another actor in the film.[5]

As Frears remembers, though, Springsteen was really, really nervous to shoot his scene. Again, that does make sense. This was his first time actually acting on film. Even if he was playing himself, a role one imagines he would know pretty well by that point, everything was scripted.

Still, he managed to comfortably settle into things within the scene. More than that, Springsteen even helped make one of the lines in the script better.

Says Pink,

> The line was "You'll feel better and they'll feel better, and you'll be able to move on." Bruce says to us, "Well, this is all great and I'm happy to do this. But you can't really say that they'll feel better. You don't really know that they'll feel better." And so he

changed the line. In the movie he says, "You'll feel better and then they'll feel better . . . maybe."[6]

During the scene, Bruce is playing a guitar that was on set. This was an idea that came from Stephen Frears as a way to help settle his nerves and make him more comfortable delivering lines on camera. After all, he's an artist, not necessarily an actor.

But then for some of the people in the room, they started seeing all the logistical issue once he started playing the guitar. Since he was playing, it was now officially a Bruce Springsteen song, and there was no way they could ever afford a Bruce Springsteen song in the movie. Immediately, dollar signs and red flags started to flash.

Steve Pink walked over to Stephen Frears and let him know the issue. Frears's response was simple. He told Pink plainly to go deal with it. So Steve Pink took a deep breath and did just that.

> I remember going up to Springsteen and saying, "Excuse me, Mr. Springsteen, God almighty, but you're playing guitar and you know how it's a movie and can we use the stuff you're playing?" I remember fumbling through the request. And I remember him saying, "Yeah, I'm not even playing anything. I'm just improvising. This is just improvising."[7]

In the end, they still needed concrete proof. So they wound up rolling film on Springsteen saying to the camera that he's only noodling around on the guitar and that they have permission to use that music in the film. Eventually, they also secured written permission from his manager.

Springsteen was with the team for no longer than a half hour in that New York studio. Still, he was kind enough to indulge the crew with a makeshift mini concert. At one point, Seamus McGarvey mentioned that his favorite album was *Nebraska*, so naturally the Boss played a song on that album for him.

The scene works brilliantly in the finished product. Bruce Springsteen's acting debut is flawless. By the time the film came out, his legend was already so big that there would be audible gasps when he came on screen. Not only did he deliver a performance, he gave the film an added layer of credibility in the music world.

After all, how many films ever get the blessing of Bruce Springsteen?

"I met him again a couple of years ago at the premiere of *Nocturnal Animals*, this film I shot with Tom Ford," says McGarvey. "And I went up to him and I said, 'Bruce Springsteen, we did *High Fidelity*.' And he said, 'I *love* that film. More people ask me about that fucking movie than they ask me about my music!'"[8]

The Springsteen sequence is one of two music-related sequences that completely manages to walk off with the film. Of course, the second sequence is courtesy of Jack Black.

Throughout the film, Barry is eager to prove to everyone that he is more than just a music snob. He wants to show the world that he is a talented musician in his own right. It's the sort of frustration that many of us have felt.

How much do you want to bet that 75 percent of the people you encounter in record stores aren't just music lovers, but also at some point had their own aspirations of music glory? Nobody wants to just sit around and listen to music. Everyone wants to make it for a living.

In the latter half of the film, Barry is on a quest to prove the naysayers, namely Rob, wrong. He manages to join a band, complete with a revolving door of names, and Laura books the band for Rob's record release party—much to Rob's chagrin. Despite Rob's repeated attempts to have Barry back out, even offering him incredible sums of money to do so, Barry is determined. He needs this chance to win everyone over, a chance to show Rob what he's capable of and that he's not just all talk.

But also, deep down, you get the sense that there's some insecurity there behind the blatant arrogance. You get the sense that Barry needs to prove to himself what he can do just as much. Consequently, the same could also be said about Jack Black.

Originally in the script it was written that Barry would sing Marvin Gaye's "Got to Give It Up." However, Jack felt that was not enough of a showstopper for the film's grand finale. If he was going to sing Marvin Gaye, it *had* to be "Let's Get It On." He had to stop the show, and with "Let's Get It On," that's exactly what he could accomplish. DeVincentis and Cusack immediately agreed, and thus the change was made.

"I was really appreciative of them letting me call my shot," remembers Black, "because it was kind of like *This isn't a karaoke bar. This is a major motion picture. They're going to let me fucking take the reins and make the call on what song I want to sing*, which was very cool of them to trust in me to do that."[9]

When it came to planning the big scene, it would be filmed at Chicago's famed Double Door. The entire sequence would be filmed in one day, with production scheduled to start for the day at 9 a.m. Jack Black had some concerns about performing that early, so Kathy Nelson wanted to have him prerecord the song so he could lip-sync.

DeVincentis wanted to put together an actual killer band to play with Jack so he once again turned to the ever-valuable asset that was Dan Koretzky. They wound up putting together a band that featured some Drag City artists from that era, including Rian Murphy, Jeff Parker, and Matt Lux. To record the song, they went to a recording studio owned by Steve Albini, whom DeVincentis had known since he was a teenager and Albini was in his early twenties.

Albini has a rich history as both a musician and a record producer, however Albini is not a fan of being credited for the latter. He prefers to not be credited on the album itself, but when he must be, he prefers to be credited as the recording engineer.

Onstage, he has played in bands such as Big Black and Flour, and he currently is a member of Shellac. He has engineered thousands of records. Most notably he worked with Nirvana on their *Nevermind* follow-up *In Utero*. You can only imagine the music legends that have graced his studio. So *High Fidelity* was in great company.

With the song prerecorded, it was finally the big day. Initially, they had Black lip-syncing. But something felt off with the first take.

"Jack Black actually couldn't lip-sync," Nelson recalled. "He couldn't do it exactly the same way twice, which would've meant they wouldn't be able to edit."[10]

After that first take with Jack lip-syncing, it was decided that he needed to sing live. The band they had backing him up was the same one they had from the recording studio, so this could be accomplished.

When you see someone singing on-screen, very rarely is it ever being done live. This is for a variety of reasons, such as having to create a consistency between takes in editing. More often than not, when you're watching someone singing in a movie, the performance is being lip-synched.

There are famous examples of other performers who had difficulty lip-syncing on-screen. Going back to *The Blues Brothers*, Aretha Franklin also struggled with this. Like Black, she had trouble singing a song the same way twice. When you watch her sing "Think" in the film, you can even notice some slight inconsistencies where it doesn't totally match up.

Jack Black, however, recalls that he wasn't going—to use his own shower-chanting mantra—"All the fucking wayyyyyy." He felt that there was something holding him back on that first take. Frears was quick to correct it, albeit in a not-so-direct approach. Black puts it like this.

Stephen Frears said, "Cut! Cut! What the *fuck* is going on here?" And he comes up and he's just ripping into the audience, that they're not enjoying it enough. They're not explosive enough. "You need to *cheer*! This music is *fantastic*!" And he's yelling at them, but I feel like really, he is yelling at me. But he didn't say anything to me. He turned to me and said, "Great job, Jack. Let's do it again."[11]

Black continues,

> I knew by the way he was frustrated with the audience for not being more into it. I knew *Oh. That's me. If I fucking rock it hard enough, they will be into it. It's my fault that they weren't into it.* Whatever it was, it did the trick. Because the next take, I fucking uncorked it. And we got the take that was in the movie. And it was just me using all of my fucking throat muscle powers and I really belted it out.

It worked. The next take was the charm. Jack Black sang live straight through and gave Barry the big moment that he desperately needed. But in the process, it also gave Jack Black the performance that he needed to bring him to the next stage of his career.

By the time the movie came out, there was no question who Jack Black was. Despite his attempts to keep his head down, here he was, firmly standing in the spotlight.

"I remember when we shot that scene," Black says.

> I was like *Mm. That felt good. I'm really glad we got that.* When I can really rock and I can feel good with the audience, that's a special moment that's not easy to capture on camera. Because once the cameras are rolling it, it puts another layer of sort of pressure that makes it hard to rock. But it felt like *Oh. That was a lucky little lightning in a bottle moment for me.*[12]

"Jack gave it his all," McGarvey recalls. "I've done a lot of music videos. I've toured with the Stones. I've shot thousands of concerts and music videos. But that was the best gig I was ever at because the crowd went mental."[13]

Back to the Boss. Bruce Springsteen's cameo was the final thing that they needed to pick up for the film. While in New York, the studio questioned Frears on whether or not he was actually finished with the film.

"The studio was questioning if I finished," says Frears. "I think they just assumed *Oh, he's probably going to want to go back and we can't stop him.*"[14]

Frears, who didn't even know him not being done with the film was a possibility at that point, was in fact done. Regardless of what the studio thought, he had everything he needed. So with that, Frears, the film's editor Mick Audsley, and eventually DeVincentis, Pink, and Cusack, jumped across the Atlantic to start the editing process.

9

Finding the Music (or the Misery?)

Stephen Frears got his wish of wanting to make sure it wasn't "too hot or too cold" while filming *High Fidelity*. After a brief stop in New York to shoot Bruce Springsteen's cameo, Frears headed back to England with the film's editor, Mick Audsley.

Audsley had worked with Frears many times before. Their director-editor relationship first started in 1982 with the TV movie *Walter* followed by *Walter & June* a year later. They went on to further work together on *The Hit*; *My Beautiful Laundrette*; *Prick Up Your Ears*; *Sammy and Rosie Get Laid*; *Dangerous Liaisons*; *The Grifters*; *Hero*; and *The Van*.

As was the case with Cusack, Bevan, and Simmons, Frears wanted to make sure he had a blend of new folks—like DeVincentis, Pink, and McGarvey—and familiar faces he had worked with previously.

Simmons says,

> If a director doesn't have an editor that they like working with, I'm used to going through a whole interview process to find somebody that they like. And then that person may be involved a week or two before. But Stephen sent every version of the script to Mick, and they talked about it. And Mick had an enormous amount of input, which is the way that directors and editors should work. They're such an important part of it.[1]

During filming in Chicago, Audsley had set up shop in a make-shift cutting room not far from the Double Door. For various reasons, Audsley's usual assistant couldn't work on the film, so he wound up using a local crew, most of which he says became "dear friends."

"I was very happy cutting there and working there," Audsley recalls. "I was living close to Stephen, so we used to meet pretty much every night, after he had been shooting, with John, Steve, or D.V., and just look at the film. We used to look at what we had done on the weekends."[2]

Having Audsley on-site and cutting during filming actually came in handy, because Frears could then go back and try to improve things. Just as how Frears felt the script was never done, if he wasn't quite happy with how a scene came out, they'd go back and pick it up again during production. "I think we can do that better. We'll have another go at it," he'd say.[3]

"I had a long-standing relationship with Stephen," Audsley adds. "There was a close language. We kind of all knew what we were going for. And I was lucky. I could hang on to their shirt tails and enjoy the ride."[4]

After filming had wrapped, there was already an assembly of the film compiled. Frears and Audsley flew to England to work on the director's cut of the film for the next five weeks. They landed on cutting in Somerset, which was not too far from where they both lived at the time. They were later joined by DeVincentis, Pink, and Cusack.

They had set things up in what DeVincentis recalls as being a "beautiful Georgian mansion in the countryside that was owned by an eccentric man named Harry." Due to its rather remote location, the only place nearby was a hotel in Taunton, which he admits was by no means a four-star town.[5]

"It was like a broken-down *Downton Abbey*, and we were cutting in like the basement," recalls Pink. "It was fucking freezing."[6]

As anyone in the industry can attest to, having writers present in the editing room is very uncommon. This is usually when the director will continue to grab hold of the reins and work very closely with the editor to bring the vision they have in their head to life. There's not a lot of room for collaboration beyond that in most cases.

However, Stephen Frears is clearly not like most directors. He encourages having that sort of collaborative environment where the writers are welcome to be in the room during editing and he can hear any and all passionate arguments that arise throughout the process.

DeVincentis recalls,

> If you see something a certain way, and it's different than what he's done and how he sees it, his response is "Alright. I'm gonna go read a book and take a walk and I'll see you tomorrow afternoon and [you can] show me how you like it. You sit with Mick and you take the reins and you do a cut of that scene the way you want it." Stephen was fine with that. Then he comes back and he looks at it. If he likes it better, that's what's in. If he doesn't, it's not what's in. But he gives you the shot.[7]

"Stephen Frears obviously had the last word on the cuts," adds Pink. "But the fact that he let us go and torture Mick Audsley, I don't know if he enjoyed the fact that we were going to go and torture Mick? I think Mick Audsley enjoyed the process, but still, it's odd when you have the writers and star in the editing room and we're cutting film."[8]

As far as Audsley is concerned, however, this was all about Frears "being fastidious about ensuring everybody was happy." He feels Frears wanted to generously make sure everyone was included throughout the editing process. That's what Audsley thinks it all boils down to.[9]

When you are working in an environment such as that with so many people involved in the editing process, passionate arguments are the norm. It'd be impossible for that to not be the case.

One instance in particular was a cut from one scene to another. In the first scene, Barry is singing "The Night Chicago Died" but changing the lyrics to sing "The Night Laura's Daddy Died." In an adlibbed moment, Rob grabs Barry and starts slapping him.

Frears suggested having it cut from that moment with Barry getting slapped to Laura's dad's funeral. Cusack and Pink thought it was hilarious. DeVincentis did not.

"I was like 'This doesn't make sense,'" DeVincentis recalls. "And I was totally wrong. It was perfect. It was great. When I sat and watched the movie and I heard other people laughing at it, that's it."[10]

Nick Hornby has said that because they were editing in London, this allowed Hornby to be able to come by and see new cuts of the film. Hornby said he was fielding calls asking him to come by to see the new cuts.

"They have this thing, I think, film people," Hornby said in an interview.

> The slightest change, and they think it's a different movie. They kept phoning up and saying, "We've taken a minute out. You've got to come down. It's a completely different story." Then you get there, and it's thirty seconds shorter and you don't notice any difference whatsoever.[11]

Hanging up in the editing room was a sign that said *You've got to have good reason to keep people there longer than 110 minutes.* This was something that Frears was very conscious of, according to Audsley. He was always trying to get the film down to "the absolute nuts and bolts."[12]

The film wound up eventually clocking in at 113 minutes. This means that if the audience got bored after 110 minutes, at least it would be during the closing credits. There was no harm in having them walk out once the film itself was over.

When you've got a film like *High Fidelity*, there's a lot riding on the soundtrack. You can't have a movie about music obsessives and have the film's music being lackluster. Music was one of the film's key components, naturally. But when it came to the soundtrack, Stephen Frears left the selections in the hands of the others. DeVincentis, Pink, and Cusack clearly knew that world and knew what they wanted.

"Ask me about early Elvis, I'll tell you everything," says Frears. "I didn't know about it in any scholarly detail. I used to say, 'You choose the music, and I'll be the judge if it goes in the film.'"

"This film couldn't be made by someone who knew about music," Frears adds. "Because they'd never have settled on anything."[13]

Frears makes a good point. The discussions about the needle drops were seemingly endless as it stood. Audsley reckons that it was probably thirty to forty weeks worth of postproduction before they got done with the music portion. Not only did that include deciding on a song that works, but also making sure that song could be cleared. Imagine how long that'd take with another music obsessive in the room.

Having Frears as an unbiased party when it came to music choices certainly helped. That way, the focus would be less on what bands he wanted to highlight and more about what specific song would help move the narrative forward. As much thought as went into every song, not to mention the many arguments he surely heard about each song, at the end of the day, it needs to work for the story. Frears could help make sure that was at the forefront of every decision.

There are two different types of songs that are present in the film. First are the songs that are actually playing within the world. This includes Dick playing "Seymour Stain" by Belle & Sebastian or Barry playing "Walking on Sunshine" as part of his Monday morning mix tape. This also includes the covers in the movie such as Marie singing Peter Frampton's "Baby I Love Your Way" or Barry's "Let's Get it On."

Then there are what are known as the needle drops. At the time the film was made, *High Fidelity* had more music cues in it than any other movie in Disney history. This was despite the fact that the budget for music that they had was less than that of *Grosse Pointe Blank*, a movie that also had a great soundtrack but *wasn't* about music obsessives.

The film's soundtrack artists reads like a who's who for any music obsessive. It includes Liz Phair; Elton John; 13th Floor Elevator; Joan Jett; Ann Peebles; Barry White; the Velvet Underground; Aretha Franklin; the Beta Band; Queen; Elvis Costello; Bob Dylan; Harry Nilsson; the Kinks; Stevie Wonder; and so many more.

Of course, there had to be a proper representation of Chicago's thriving music scene. In this case, it helped to have someone like Dan Koretzky from Drag City Records as a close friend to the production.

"They had all kinds of different song needs, and if Drag City was able to fill it, we wanted to square peg the fuck outta that round hole shit," said Koretzkty.

> We ended up not only getting a good bit of our music in the soundtrack but also some of our musicians (Liam Hayes from Plush, Rian Murphy from Chestnut Station, Al Johnson from US Maple) in the actual film as well. Not to mention the great Jeff Parker and Matt Lux—such incredible musical talent put to such little use![14]

Everyone had their own take on what songs should go where and was fully prepared to justify why their take on a scene was better than everyone else's. That was bound to happen in this sort of environment. Fortunately things never got *too* heated in the process. Or at least if they did, nobody can really remember specifics.

"We had epic battles, and I found them to be enjoyable epic battles, by the way," Pink recalls.

> It could be frustrating at times and angry at times, and that person's a fucking idiot to want that song in the movie or vice versa. We were mirroring the characters in the movie in that superior way of *We know what the music for the movie should be and everyone else who thinks it should be something else is a fucking idiot.*[15]

"I could definitely go to fucking war for a song in a movie," adds DeVincentis. "I could be at war with somebody who I would also throw myself in front of a bus for. It was spirited and there was a lot of refereeing to be done. Various people traded off being the referee, including myself."[16]

As Mike Newell recalls, when he worked with Cusack on *Pushing Tin*, he got a glimpse into what it might have been like to work with him on *High Fidelity* when it came to music.

> There was an issue with what other kinds of music did that character listen to. We had several discussions about this, at the end of which I said to myself, *I'm going to set aside however much time it takes and I will listen to every piece of music that John wants me to listen to.*[17]

Newell wound up spending nearly two days listening to all the music Cusack provided him with, and all for just one scene. You can imagine just how his approach intensified when it came to working on a film like *High Fidelity* where the soundtrack is so crucial.

Yes, Cusack was just as passionate as anyone when it came to what music made its way into the movie. At one point during the postproduction process, Cusack had to fly back to Los Angeles. After about five hours, Mick Audsley got a phone call from Cusack. Turns out Cusack had used his star power to talk his way into the cockpit to use the pilot's phone to call Audsley with a new song pitch.

"It's like John's character," says Simmons of the music process.

> You're putting together the perfect mix tape. And that's what
> *High Fidelity* is. It's the perfect mix-tape. But it's a perfect mix
> tape that's being made by four or five creative individuals, and
> who knows how many studio execs. So it took a while to kind of
> find what everybody wanted.[18]

As hard as it was to decide on what music was right for the film, as well as what song should go where, that wasn't the only obstacle at play. Once everyone decided on a song they wanted—or the majority ruled at the very least—there was also the question of clearance.

Those outside of business may not realize just how difficult securing a specific song can be. Between the asking price of the artist or the holder of the music rights being too high or perhaps just not hearing back about a certain song, there's a ton of negotiating that goes into getting the perfect song for your soundtrack.

Luckily, *High Fidelity* had Kathy Nelson as their music supervisor. She is known in the industry for making miracles happen when it comes to your film's soundtrack. If there's a song you want, Kathy Nelson will do *whatever* it takes to make it so, guaranteed.

A particular instance of Nelson's dedication came when they were in London working on the film. Nelson was in the middle of a dinner meeting, and at one point crawled underneath the table to call DeVincentis in London.

According to DeVincentis, she told him, "If you will just put this particular song in the movie, because it's on Hollywood Records and Hollywood Records is Hollywood Pictures and it's all in the family, it'll give you so much wiggle room."[19]

"You can have it playing out of a radio," Nelson added, according to DeVincentis. "It doesn't matter."

"It says a lot about Kathy," DeVincentis says. "She's looking out for us. She's looking after us. She's also covering our ass by getting us to do something that we should just fucking do."[20]

"I think the editor said to me at that point that he'd never had to load so much music into his Avid ever," says Nelson. "It was probably one of the most fun movies I'd ever gotten to work on."[21]

The movie, much like the book, is filled to the brim with so many things that, if you've ever worked in a record store, hit incredibly close to home. One such moment comes during the busy Saturday sequence where we see Rob bet Dick that he can get three people to buy a copy of the Beta Band simply by playing it in the store. Ask anyone who has worked the counter at a record store, and they will assure you that this does work.

For that scene, DeVincentis, Pink, and Cusack knew that they wanted to find something that 99 percent of the audience would not recognize, because they wanted it to genuinely feel like Rob was introducing them to something that they hadn't heard before, just as he was doing in the film. Whenever something like this would arise, DeVincentis turned to the person he knew would have the perfect solution for them: Dan Koretzky.

In the film, they used the song "Dry the Rain" by the Beta Band. But more than just that, at one point there was even talk of having them score the film.

DeVincentis recalls meeting with them in New York. They had dinner, DeVincentis caught their show, and the band seemed really into the idea. However, slowly but surely they started backing out of the project. At the time nobody knew why.

Later on, DeVincentis found out that this was because the lead singer Steve Mason was having struggles with his mental health at the time. This resulted in the band having conflicts and eventually breaking up in 2004.

The film itself has over fifty needle drops and songs featured. The film is literally wall-to-wall with great music throughout. That being said, there were some sections of the film that still needed to be scored.

DeVincentis recalls,

> Frears said, "I've let all of you young people run wild. You guys and Seamus." Like many things that Stephen says, it's half joking and half serious. He was like, "You young people have run amuck. I'm going to take a run at this score with somebody my age." I said, "I think Howard's actually younger than you." He's like, "No matter!"[22]

Howard, in this instance, was the legendary Howard Shore. Even though it was a year before his work on *Lord of the Rings*, something he will forever be identified with, Shore had built up a steady stream of successes as one of the best composers working in Hollywood.

Shore first came to prominence as the musical director for *Saturday Night Live* when the show launched in 1975. In the 1980s, he turned to composing for films such as *After Hours*; *The Fly*; and *Big*. His success in film continued in the 1990s with projects like *The Silence of the Lambs*; *Mrs. Doubtfire*; *Philadelphia*; *Ed Wood*; *That Thing You Do!*; and *Dogma*. From his previous credits alone, Shore would certainly be a big get for any film.

"Howard understands movies in such a sophisticated manner," says Audsley. "We can only watch in admiration from the sidelines."[23]

Again, with so many great songs and artists already being featured, very little score would actually be needed for the film.

DeVincentis recalls, "You know Howard Shore's a brilliant guy.
He's the best. I want to say at the top that this was a mountain made
out of a mole hill. There's very little score in the movie. It's not a make
or break thing for the movie. It's wall-to-wall needle drops."

DeVincentis continues,

> I got next to Howard, and I was like, "Your music is so great.
> I just think some things need to be moved around. Maybe a
> different voice in there. Maybe less electric piano or something.
> I don't know." And he was like, "Look, I agree. But I have to get
> on a plane right now to New Zealand to start *Lord of the Rings*.
> So I can't do anything."[24]

After this, DeVincentis got permission from Frears to try an
alternative. There was an instrumental record Drag City put out by
Papa M, a one-man project by David Pajo of Slint and Tortoise fame.
DeVincentis felt the record might be a good fit for *High Fidelity*. So
DeVincentis and music editor Mike Higham spent a few days build-
ing an alternative score out of the record.

They went back and showed the cut with the new score to Frears,
Audsley, and the mixers. The room was mixed, saying, "It could be
either one." Finally Frears made the decision. "Well fine. Let's just put
this one in."[25]

With that, the journey of *High Fidelity*'s postproduction was finally
at the end. Champagne was popped on the mixing stage. The last thing
that had to be done was the Dolby mix, which didn't require anything
other than the man from Dolby moving around some of the Dolby
knobs. Beyond that, they were done. So DeVincentis flew home.

When he landed, he was told that Frears had decided to put
Shore's score back in the film. At the last minute, they reverted it

back, which was fine as they had already done a mix to it. So that was the version they did the final Dolby mix to, all while DeVincentis was flying back to Los Angeles.

"Boo hoo," DeVincentis mockingly laments. "I was so upset about it. Now I see it really doesn't matter. Howard's music is wonderful, graceful, and doesn't compete with the needle-drops. He really knew what he was doing and it shows."[26]

Back in the United States, the film had a test screening in Pasadena. The screening performed quite well. But for Audsley, it also told him of changes that still needed to be made.

"I remember because of the comedic nature it was extraordinarily helpful to me from an editorial point of view," Audsley says. "Because when you hear people laughing, you need to tune the speed of the film very carefully."[27]

There was one moment in particular, however, he knew he had to keep adjusting. The fantasy fight sequence where Rob, Dick, and Barry beat up Ian in the record and Dick subsequently bludgeons him with the air conditioning unit was one of the biggest laughs of the film. The laughs were so big that Audsley had to keep adding more and more footage of Rob walking up to Charlie's apartment. This was because the laughs kept drowning out the return of Catherine Zeta-Jones in the film.

One thing that Frears recalls about the test screenings is the response he got from the studio afterward.

"I remember Disney said to me, 'Can't you marry him at the end?'" Frears recalls. "I said, 'Well no.' And then when we showed it, people would say, 'What's great is that it doesn't have a Hollywood ending.' I don't think it would've helped one iota."[28]

Everything was now locked in with the film and it was ready to roll out. Well, almost . . .

10

Written by D.V. DeVincentis, Steve Pink, and John Cusack & Scott Rosenberg?

Back in the mid-1990s, Scott Rosenberg opted to leave *High Fidelity* to go work on another project. However, the werewolf biker film he set out to work on with Wes Craven never wound up happening. When Rosenberg was working on the project, Craven was just coming off the commercial failure that was *Vampire in Brooklyn*. Craven's track record changed in 1996. Craven was on top of the world again after the massive success that *Scream* wound up becoming.

After that, Rosenberg wound up writing *Con Air*, which coincidentally starred John Cusack. He also wrote the psychological horror film *Disturbing Behavior* and was the ninth writer attached to *Armageddon*, for which he did uncredited rewrites.

In the meantime, *High Fidelity* was rewritten from scratch by DeVincentis, Pink, and Cusack. After his relationship with the film ended, Rosenberg had no other involvement. According to DeVincentis, in passing they were told that there was a draft written by Rosenberg "but they wanted to start over from scratch, and there was no value in reading it." So with that, they got to work on the film and they never gave another thought to what had happened before they were involved.[1]

Before a film is released, everything needs to be finalized and approved by the parties involved. This includes the credits that will be associated with the film. Typically, the process is pretty standard, where you'd maybe have to correct the spelling of a name here or there. But usually, there's nothing really out of the ordinary.

As the filmmakers were finalizing the credits, DeVincentis, Pink, and Cusack received paperwork from the Writer's Guild of America (WGA) with a list of possible arbitrations. On that list was Scott Rosenberg's name.

According to the WGA website, an "arbitration is similar to a civil trial. Instead of a judge or jury, a neutral arbitrator will be selected to hear and decide this dispute. Most MBA arbitrators have years of experience handling disputes under the Guild agreement."[2]

Essentially, this would mean that Rosenberg would be up for a writing credit on a film that didn't use anything from his draft. DeVincentis, Pink, and Cusack had never even read his draft up to this point. The reason he was up for credit was because he was the first writer attached to the project. Whether or not anything from his draft was used didn't matter. As the first writer, anything that he incorporated—even if he took it directly from the book—was now considered his contribution to the first draft.

"It used to be that the first writer of any adaptation would get full credit for anything they extracted from the book, or from the material from which they were adapting," says Pink of the WGA rules that have now changed. "So any subsequent writer would not get credit for it. If there was a gas station in the novel and you also put the gas station in the novel, you don't get credit for it. The first writer gets credit for it, even though the gas station itself is in the novel."[3]

As for what was going on with *High Fidelity*, DeVincentis, Pink, and Cusack were confused. Nobody had been expecting to see his name on the list. Once they received the list with Scott's name attached as a potential arbitration, Cusack decided to give him a call. So the three of them all got on the phone and called Scott Rosenberg, who was staying in a house that he'd rented with some friends on Martha's Vineyard.

Rosenberg says he remembers every detail of that call vividly because for him it came out of left field entirely. The feeling was mutual. It was also an out-of-left-field experience for DeVincentis, Pink, and Cusack.

As DeVincentis recalls of the phone call, "Scott said, 'Oh yeah. I did a draft. But I saw your draft, I saw the movie, and obviously nothing of mine is in the movie. I'll make sure my name's not on there, because I'm not trying to get credit for it. I totally understand it's not mine.'"[4]

Rosenberg, however, says that he never offered to call anyone to get his name removed.

> They called and they were like, "You don't deserve credit." I was like, "Okay. What do you mean I don't deserve credit?" And that's when they said, "Well, we never looked at your draft." I said, "Okay. But what do you want me to do?" They were producers and Johnny was a star. It's an automatic arbitration.[5]

A week later, DeVincentis, Pink, and Cusack got an updated list of possible arbitrations. Lo and behold, Rosenberg's name was still on there. They called him up immediately. This time, they were even more confused. They thought everyone was on the same page after that first call. That didn't seem to be the case.

DeVincentis recalls,

> We were on speaker from John's office. We get a hold of him and were like, "Hey, um, dude, your name is still on this credit arbitration thing. Did you call somebody yet to let them know to take it off?" And he goes, "Yeah . . . Actually I was talking to my lawyer," which is never a good start for anything, "and he told

me that because of the way the Writer's Guild rules are, I actually have a really good shot of getting a credit on the movie."[6]

As one could imagine, this is the part where things go from just being weird to being tense, even borderline heated.

"Ask anyone who knows me, I don't listen to my lawyers," Rosenberg says. "It's just not who I am. Don't blame a lawyer. It was my decision. It's just really not that big a deal. It's like, 'You guys can't say I don't deserve credit because you haven't read my draft.'"[7]

According to Rosenberg, he says that he was never going to go to the WGA and advocate to receive credit. But he also wasn't going to go and say he didn't deserve credit. One of the biggest sticking points for Rosenberg, to this day, is the fact that they never read his draft up until it got to this point.

"If a writer that you like wrote the first draft, why wouldn't you even look at it?" Rosenberg argues. "I'm not saying my script was the greatest thing in the world, but wouldn't you read it? Especially if it was someone who wrote your biggest grossing movie?"[8]

That last part is, of course, a reference to the fact that he and Cusack had worked together on *Con Air*. It's just another weird coincidence in this incredibly weird story.

"Cusack was my buddy," says Rosenberg. "We hung out. We were friends. Then when I found out they were doing [*High Fidelity*], I was delighted. *Grosse Pointe Blank* was amazing. This [was] absolutely great news. And I thought it was going to be a big happy ending."[9]

"He knows very well why we didn't read the draft," says Pink.

Just on a very basic level, Joe Roth handed us the book and he didn't like the draft, and he wanted us to start over. To do a pure adaptation. So at that point, why would we read the other draft?[10]

While on the phone with them, Rosenberg offered up that he knew how it felt. He had been on their side of the table while working on *The General's Daughter*. Rosenberg had done a rewrite on the film, but the first writer got all the credit. Rosenberg argued that he was willing to share credit with DeVincentis, Pink, and Cusack.

"I worked on the movie. I adapted the book," Rosenberg says.

> The one thing I'm not going to do is send a letter saying *I absolutely don't deserve credit*. And they were like, "Why would you ever want credit on something you never worked on?" But I did work on it. If the studio had said, "It's John, D.V., and Steve," I certainly wouldn't have fought it. I would've accepted it. But in this case, it was going to arbitration.[11]

"He fully acknowledged to us that we didn't use any of his material and you'd only have to look at his own script and our script to know that," says Pink. "It's no secret. You could probably find his script and read our script and find that they don't resemble each other at all."[12]

At this point, Rosenberg was telling DeVincentis, Pink, and Cusack that if he really wanted to, there was a good chance that he could get sole credit for *High Fidelity*. Instead, he was suggesting that instead they all just share credit.

Rosenberg insists that he doesn't see what the big deal was. But for DeVincentis, Pink, and Cusack, they had spent years of their lives working on this very personal experience.

"It's like we all went to the moon, and then we came back and then Scott Rosenberg said he was on the moon with us," jokes Pink.

> It's like, *We don't understand how you could say you were on the moon with us even if you wrote a book about the moon*. Even if you looked at the moon, you weren't on the moon with us. And we didn't even use your map to get to the moon. We didn't use your spaceship, we didn't use your telescope, and then we get

to the moon and we hang out on the moon, and then we come back from the moon and you said you went on the moon with us.[13]

DeVincentis remembers,

I told Rosenberg that I would be willing to meet him in his lawyer's office and sign over all my residuals for the movie to him, in perpetuity, if he would just take his name out of this because as he said, he had nothing to do with writing this film.[14]

Steve Pink also offered up all his residuals, which he looks back in horror at nowadays. Cusack offered up his as well. Rosenberg says, "Not in a million years did that ever happen."[15]

At this point in the phone call with the trio, he reportedly lost his temper. He said, "What's so wrong with sharing a credit with me? Are you embarrassed to share a credit with me?" Cusack, who has a knack for keeping his cool in these situations, said, "No, Scott, not at all. Let's write a movie together and share credit. But not this one, because as you said, you contributed nothing to this movie."[16]

Rosenberg says that he feels today that this entire incident was blown way out of proportion, "You genuinely would've thought that I'd kidnapped the Lindbergh baby, committed the Manson murders, and shot Bobby Kennedy by how fucking wrong these guys were."[17]

In accordance with WGA rules at the time, Rosenberg was therefore credited for the film. The film is credited to D.V. DeVincentis, Steve Pink, and John Cusack & Scott Rosenberg. While the average filmgoer may not notice it, anyone who knows the story can tell the ampersand is basically a line in the sand between DeVincentis, Pink, and Cusack, and Scott Rosenberg.

Pink recalls Rosenberg saying,

Well, it's just business, guys. This is how it works. You always arbitrate for credit because it means money. It doesn't even matter whether you believe you deserve credit. I wrote a draft and I respect that you guys wrote a different draft and that they may not resemble each other, but this is just how the business works.[18]

"In hindsight," says Rosenberg, "if I had to do it all over again, I can't tell you I would do it any differently. It is what it is. I just went through this on the first *Jumanji* movie. And it wasn't that big of a deal. We shared credit with the first writers."[19]

Despite all of this, Rosenberg still holds the film in high regard. He says he really likes the film, though he is still baffled about what the big deal about everything was. Still it makes no difference. On paper, Scott Rosenberg will forever have his name attached to *High Fidelity*.

At the end of the day, that was Scott Rosenberg's only contribution to the world of *High Fidelity*. Well, for now, at least.

11

The Release

It took nearly five years to get from the book being optioned to it finally hitting the big screen. This is not uncommon in the world of film. Despite being optioned before the book ever hit shelves, the option is only the beginning of the long, treacherous journey. There're so many more factors that come into play the majority of people—both audience members and young authors—wouldn't suspect. There're more ways that it could not pan out than it could pan out.

In many ways, the option is indeed the easiest part of the process. The hard part is everything that comes after it. You could open hundreds of bookstores and it still wouldn't be enough to contain all the books that have been optioned for film rights that never saw the light of day. Hell, most of them never even made it to preproduction. And you could also have an entire section of books that were optioned but never even had a script produced before they were just abandoned unceremoniously.

Nevertheless, despite all the stress that went into preproduction, production, and the long postproduction stage, it thankfully had a happy ending. Everyone involved got to make the movie they wanted to make, and now it was finally coming out.

High Fidelity had its world premiere at the famed SXSW Festival in Austin, Texas. The film premiered on March 17 at a special screening that was held outside the narrative competition. However, neither DeVincentis or Pink have any recollection of attending the festival for the premiere. They weren't even sure that the film even played there. But it did, indeed, happen.[1]

On March 31, 2000, *High Fidelity* hit theaters in the United States. But before that, of course, there was the traditional big Hollywood premiere. The film's premiere was held at the famed El Capitan Theater in Hollywood. In addition to the cast and crew, the film was attended by other notable celebrities including Richard Dreyfus, Malcolm McDowell, Sam Elliot, Jason Lee, Robert Wagner, Jeremy Piven, and even George Clooney.

Says Black,

> I was talking to my mom and she was just like glowing after the movie. She was so happy. And then up walks motherfucking George Clooney, and he was like, "Jack, that was fucking amazing, man. You're great in this movie." And he left and my mom was just like slack jawed. She couldn't fucking believe it.[2]

Steve Pink had really hoped that *High Fidelity* would be a fall release, however. It wasn't a strategic approach, as far as wanting to have the film open up during a certain weekend where it would best perform. He just had certain nostalgic feelings about Chicago in the fall, and felt it would work better as a fall movie.

Instead, we got to see *High Fidelity* in the springtime. Typically March is reserved for the lighter fare, or at least it was back then. Streaming services and superhero movies have changed all of that, and the rules are less definitive. But back then, the summer was reserved for blockbusters, and the winter was reserved for all of the Oscar hopefuls that are desperate to not miss the cutoff.

Clearly *High Fidelity* was not your summer blockbuster, nor would it do well up against them. It also came out right after the awards season ended. So it was sort of smack dab in the middle of both categorizations.

Critically, much like the book, the film was very well received. The film has a 91 percent fresh rating on Rotten Tomatoes. Despite initial fan objections to the film being moved from London to Chicago, the film really managed to strike a chord with critics.

Roger Ebert wrote,

> *High Fidelity* is a comedy about real people in real lives. The movie looks like it was easy to make—but it must not have been because movies this wry and likable hardly ever get made. Usually a clunky plot gets in the way, or the filmmakers are afraid to let their characters seem too smart. Watching *High Fidelity*, I had the feeling I could walk out of the theater and meet the same people on the street—and want to, which is an even higher compliment.[3]

In addition to being perhaps one of the most well-known film critics of that era, Ebert also was a Chicago icon, having been the lead film critic for the *Chicago Sun Times* from 1967 to 2013. So if anyone knows about how Chicago can be captured on film, it'd be him. In regard to this, Ebert wrote that the filmmakers "transplanted the story to Chicago so successfully that it feels like it grew organically out of the funky soil of Lincoln Avenue and North Halsted, Old Town and New Town, Rogers Park and Hyde Park, and Wicker Park, where it was shot."

"Despite the change of venue, the movie remains remarkably true to the novel's spirit," wrote Stephen Holden, film critic for the *New York Times*. "If the characters' musical obsessions don't precisely coincide with those of the novel, they haven't been softened. The esoterica Rob and his colleagues swap with such competitive zeal remains as specialized (and as accurate) as before."[4]

David Ansen from *Newsweek* gave the film a glowing review, while noting that the relationship between Rob and Laura was "the least compelling part of the movie."

He added that "*High Fidelity* never feels formulaic. It's an inside job, refreshingly specific. You don't feel there were armies of studio execs breathing down the filmmakers' necks, trying to reach for the lowest common denominator."[5]

The general consensus among critics was that the film managed to capture the spirit of the book. While the biggest change was the location the film was set in, few, if any, seemed to take issue with that. If anything, changing the locations was viewed as giving the film a fresh take in a way that made perfect sense in terms of the story.

Of course, the cast also got high praise. Many considered the film to be a career best for Cusack, who was riding high from the acclaim *Being John Malkovich* had received just six months earlier. It offered high hopes that Cusack would go on to keep delivering similar performances into the new millennium—something that would only be partly met.

Naturally, Jack Black felt like a discovery of sorts to many, despite the fact that he already had a rising presence thanks to Tenacious D. This film gave him further legitimacy as an actor. Many applauded not just his performance, but specifically his performance at the end. Even though anyone who knew of Tenacious D knew that he could sing, the fact that you still find yourself surprised by how good the end result is spoke volumes of Black's acting chops.

High Fidelity seemed to always be one of those movies that was destined to be passed around. The word-of-mouth feel started with the book. In the same way that Rob, Dick, and Barry would passionately tell you why their tastes were superior to yours, the film wound up getting spoken about in much of the same way. The more you heard about it, the more you felt that pull to finally check it out.

It's like the party you aren't invited to in high school. The more you hear people talking about it, the more you have to find a way to be there.

Also, comparing book sales and box office results is unfair. When you've got a book, there isn't the same type of pressure to find an audience right away.

There're no arbitrary rules saying that if a book doesn't reach a certain percentage of the audience the weekend it comes out, it's a bomb. Certainly it doesn't hurt to have good advanced book sales, but this doesn't feel as necessary as it does in the film world. Books are allowed a greater period of time to build up buzz post-release before they're considered a flop.

When you had a theatrically released film in 2000, those rules applied. A Friday, Saturday, and Sunday could make or break you. You had to prove within that very small window that at the *very* least you'd be able to clear your budget. If you failed to at least be on track for hitting that mark during your theatrical run, you were basically dead in the water, glowing reviews be damned.

In the case of *High Fidelity*, the budget was $30 million. At the very least, you had to clear that threshold in order to avoid being rendered a box office disappointment.

You also have to understand the audience that the film was made for. Despite being a commercial release by Touchstone, *High Fidelity* always had more of an art-house feel to it. Yes, you had the bankability of a movie star like John Cusack going for you. But at the time, some of the other cast members like Jack Black, Iben Hjejle, and Todd Louiso were not household names. There was a good chance you might've seen Jack on HBO with Tenacious D or maybe you saw Todd's scene in *Jerry Maguire*, but neither actor had found mainstream success yet.

Still, the book *High Fidelity* had finally found its audience in the United States five years after it was released. The book had a solid reputation in the right circles—primarily with music obsessives. So if you were a devoted fan of the book, you were likely going to be at the theater for opening weekend.

The movie was released in 1,183 theaters on opening day, which was definitely fewer than the other new films opening up that week. Among its competition was the thriller *The Skulls*, which starred Joshua Jackson and Paul Walker and was directed by Rob Cohen. Also opening that week was the Dreamworks animated musical film *The Road to El Dorado*. Obviously, there wasn't much crossover appeal going on that weekend.

All three movies, however, wound up getting their asses kicked by *Erin Brockavich*, which was in its third week by the time *High Fidelity* came out. *Erin Brockavich* finished first, raking in $13,798,460, followed by *The Road to El Dorado* which brought in $12,846,652, and *The Skulls* bringing in $11,034,885. Behind that was the martial arts action film *Romeo Must Die*, which brought in $9,378,376.[6]

As for Rob, Laura, and the gang at Championship Vinyl? They opened fifth that weekend at $6,429,107.

At least they made it to the top five. How painful would it have been if a film that so proudly showcases the notion of a top five—and even features the line "Maybe you'd sneak into the top ten, but there's just no room for you in the top five"—wasn't able to do that in its opening weekend?

"One of the things that I used to do just for the fun of it in the '90s was call Moviefone with a zip code in like Arkansas and find out what are people watching in a crazy random place like that," says Pink.

So I called and got a hold of a theater. And I go, "Hey, what's everybody watching? What's the big movie down there?" And she was like, "Oh, *Skulls*." I said, "Oh really? Everyone's watching

Skulls?" And she's like, "Oh yeah. Everyone's going to see *Skulls*."
And I was like, "What about *High Fidelity*?" And she was like,
"Nah. I mean, a little bit, but not really."[7]

In addition to the film having more of a word-of-mouth feel, you
also have to consider that it only opened on 1,183 screens. Mean-
while, all of the other films that were playing that weekend at least
doubled that.

Still, the filmmakers and everyone else involved with the movie
felt like it was a win. In a business that is renowned for its consistent
studio notes, tweaks, pitches on ways to "make things better," and
having to choose your battles, *High Fidelity* managed to sort of fly
under the radar of that sort of thing. The general consensus among
the cast and crew is that the labor of love paid off.

By the time *High Fidelity* ended its theatrical run, it had garnered
$27,287,137 at the domestic box office with $19,839,158 worldwide.
This brought its total to $47,126,295 in theaters alone. Against a bud-
get of $30 million, that's definitely a modest success. Had the film
been unable to clear its initial budget, that'd be a different story. It
may not have lit the world on fire, but it did what it had to do in
theaters.[8]

"It's a quirky little movie," producer Rudd Simmons says of its box
office appeal.

> You can't pigeonhole it. It's not really a love story. It definitely
> doesn't follow the structure of a rom-com. It's not really a music
> film. And I think that it's one of the reasons that I love the film,
> that it's a quirky little thing in and of itself.[9]

That total also doesn't count the home video release and rentals, an
area in which it did very well. Again, there was the discovery factor.
The more people hear about it, long after the movie theater popcorn

has lost its flavor, the more they'll want to seek it out. That in fact is what started the film gaining its cult status.

Given the film's critical acclaim, it's no surprise that it wound up making the rounds on the awards circuit. However, Touchstone and Working Title wound up giving the big push for all the major awards to the Coen Brothers' *O Brother, Where Art Thou?*

Still, *High Fidelity* managed to nab nominations throughout the year, including a Golden Globe nomination for John Cusack, as well as WGA Awards and BAFTA Awards nominations for the screenplay. Jack Black was also nominated for an MTV Movie Award for Breakthrough Performance and Best Music Moment along with Bruce Springsteen for Best Cameo in a Movie. None of these nominations resulted in wins.

There was an additional sting that came from the studio putting all their eggs in the basket of *O Brother, Where Art Thou?* At the BAFTAs, *O Brother, Where Art Thou?* was nominated for a Best Original Screenplay. *High Fidelity* was nominated for Best Adapted Screenplay alongside *Traffic*; *Chocolat*; *Crouching Tiger*; and *Wonder Boys*. *Almost Famous* won Best Original Screenplay, and *Traffic* won Best Adapted Screenplay.

At the Oscars, the Best Adapted Screenplay category consisted of *Traffic*; *Chocolat*; *Crouching Tiger*; *Wonder Boys*; and *O Brother, Where Art Thou?* Why did the latter make the switch to Adapted Screenplay? One can only assume it was because *Almost Famous* was clearly going to be the frontrunner (and eventual winner) of the Best Original Screenplay Oscar. Again, *Traffic* won for the Best Adaptation Oscar.

So had *O Brother, Where Art Thou?* not been nominated for Best Adapted Screenplay, one can only guess that *High Fidelity* would have, once again, snuck its way into the top five.

As much as a success as *High Fidelity* was for everybody involved, perhaps it can be argued that it did the most for Jack Black. Before the film, he definitely had underground appeal. He hadn't had that big breakout role yet. *High Fidelity* was clearly that for him.

Says Black,

> I was just fucking over-the-moon happy that it felt like I con-
> nected with a role. Because you've gotta know, I've been doing
> this since I was thirteen years old. I got my first professional job
> on a commercial way back when and little parts here and there.
> And I'd have little funny moments, and little things where it's
> like *Ah that was pretty good.* But I never had a thing where I
> really connected, and I felt like I hit a home run.[10]

Perhaps the richest irony of Jack Black insisting on auditioning for the film to prove it to himself was that he never had to audition again. After the success of *High Fidelity*, he was able to become offer only and could throw away his headshot. In his words, the game had changed.

After *High Fidelity*, Jack Black went on to star in films like *Saving Silverman*; *Shallow Hal*; and *Orange County*. In 2003, only three years removed from playing Barry, he starred in *School of Rock*, which not only earned him a Golden Globe nomination, but once again changed the game for him. He went from being recognizable to being a bona fide comedy super star. He has since followed it up with films like *Nacho Libre*; *King Kong*; *Kung Fu Panda*; *Tropic Thunder*; *Bernie*; and the popular *Jumanji* reboot. Oddly enough, the latter was written by Scott Rosenberg.

High Fidelity is also notable for Cusack as it saw him continuing his return to form in a way. Much like *Grosse Pointe Blank*, *High Fidelity* has a love story buried deep within its core. During this period, it seemed like Cusack had effectively cracked the code. He found a way to take on more interesting and challenging roles, while also finding a way to return to the more romantic, lead-type stories that audiences were expecting him to do more of after *Say Anything*.

Following *High Fidelity*, though, it seemed like Cusack further embraced the romantic comedy genre once again. In 2001, he starred in two rom-coms. The first, *America's Sweethearts*, was opposite Julia Roberts and was directed by Joe Roth. Later that year, he starred opposite Kate Beckinsale in *Serendipity*. Both of those films kicked off Cusack's return to a genre that he would continue to revisit throughout the next phase in his career.

Speaking of Cusack's career, it did take a bit of an odd turn in the mid-2000s. At this point, he started appearing in more and more straight-to-video films, before it became cool to have your movie go straight-to-VOD via a streaming service. While he would still star in the occasional blockbuster, most notably *2012*, which was torn apart by critics but did exceptionally well at the box office, Cusack was definitely heading in a different direction with his career than many would have predicted.

A common thread after any project in Hollywood is noting just how many times everyone who made the film crossed paths after it was released—sort of like the six degrees of *High Fidelity*.

Cusack and Steve Pink wound up collaborating again on *Hot Tub Time Machine*, which turned out to be a big commercial success and even spawned a sequel, sans Cusack.

DeVincentis and Pink wound up doing uncredited rewrites together on Michael Lehmann's *40 Days and 40 Nights*. DeVincentis would later team up with Frears again on the film *Lay the Favorite*. Then in 2019, Frears teamed up with Hornby on *State of the Union*.

In 2006, Frears was nominated for his second Academy Award for the critically acclaimed *The Queen*. Many other films he directed also received nominations including *Philomena*; *Dirty Pretty Things*; and *Mrs. Henderson Presents*.

In 2017, DeVincentis took home an Emmy Award for writing *The People v. OJ* and was again nominated for *Pam and Tommy*, for which he was executive producer and showrunner. Steve Pink moved to directing in 2006 with *Accepted*, followed by *Hot Tub Time Machine*, *Hot Tub Time Machine 2*, *About Last Night*, and *The Wheel*.

Todd Louiso stepped behind the camera in 2002 for *Love Liza*, which starred his former roommate, Dick-or-Barry hopeful Philip Seymour Hoffman. He followed this up with *The Marc Pease Experience* and *Hello I Must Be Going*, which was selected as the opening night film at the Sundance Film Festival that year. He also cowrote a 2015 film adaptation of *Macbeth*.

Another interesting aspect of the film is how it has been re-evaluated in recent years—specifically the character of Rob and how that character is depicted in the film.

Yes, the general discussion of Rob's character and his apparent flaws has been consistent. However, as the culture has shifted toward closely evaluating content both current and years old, the commentary on Rob and his flaws seems to be a lot louder.

One critique of the character was written for *Vice* in 2018 by Dan Ozzi. The headline puts it all on front street: "*High Fidelity* Created a Hero for a Generation of Sociopathic 'Nice Guys.'" The article was written shortly after it was announced that there would be a series based on *High Fidelity*, where Rob would now be played by a female, which Ozzi said was an odd choice "given the lead character's sense of male entitlement."[11]

Ozzi's argument is that while Hornby and the people behind the film firmly understood what an asshole Rob is, there were people in the culture who completely misinterpreted the character and romanticized him beyond what the initial intention was.

Another modern-day critique of the character was written by Scott Tobias for the *Guardian*. In his piece, he argues that the journey in *High Fidelity* follows Rob, who is a jerk, as he attempts to become a little bit less of a jerk.

Says Tobias,

> It didn't seem necessary to point that out 20 years ago, when the film received exactly the niche appreciation it was destined to find, but it does now, because it's not often we're given a hero as blinkered as Rob Gordon and not told how we're supposed to feel about him.[12]

What's most interesting about these critiques is that the majority of them are not so much critical of how the character was written or even portrayed. That's because Rob openly admits to being "a fucking asshole" in both the film and the book. He knows exactly what he is and who he is, as did Hornby and the film's screenwriters.

It's the construction of the character that makes him work. You only stick with Rob as a reader and a viewer because of just how much care went into making him compelling enough to stick with during his emotional journey.

The critiques in recent years have been about the people who are unable to pick up on the character's flaws. This is a character who is difficult and complicated and he can come across as so incredibly charming. That's really the point. It's just ironic that, somewhere down the line, this fact started going entirely over the heads of those who viewed him as an anti-hero.

Cusack, for one, actually seems pleased that people are starting to talk more about the character's flaws than they had when the film first came out.

"I'm glad that people have changed their view of Rob," Cusack said in an interview. "I mean, he was an [expletive]. We all are. If somebody was writing that Rob was a passive-aggressive womanizer, I'd be like, 'All right, somebody got it.' I *wanted* to reveal the flaws of the character."[13]

"It's a very objectionable, difficult, complex, not great person as a character," says DeVincentis.

> And John, because he's so naturally magnetic and empathetic, he's able to play these roles and find so much dimension and range in them and the audience is still with him and still likes this character, despite the fact that the character is kind of awful.[14]

Pink concurs that having someone as "charming and warm" as Cusack allowed them to get away with writing a character that he describes as "the worst person on the fucking planet." They were looking to show someone was deeply flawed and complicated as a human being, because that can be said about everyone.[15]

High Fidelity is perhaps the greatest representation of John Cusack's power to bring charm to any character. In the hands of someone who lacks that natural charm, it's more than just making Rob look like an asshole. Even with Cusack playing Rob, we still know what an asshole he is.

So Cusack brought an empathy to the role that it's hard to say another actor would've been capable of bringing. That's because the empathy had to appear effortless. While we do see Rob taking steps to try to overcome his flaws and obstacles, it's not as if those steps are big swings. The steps are as simple as not cheating on your girlfriend with the journalist who is interviewing you.

With Cusack at the helm, this still plays as a victory for the character. You find yourself getting lost with the character and wanting to see him succeed at the end. When he does more or less have that success, you're cheering him on every step of the way. Even more, you feel genuine happiness for this character. A character who, mind you, borrowed money from his pregnant girlfriend that he cheated on that he never intended to pay back.

It's not so much the character that you find yourself identifying with, but rather John Cusack by way of Rob. That may be where some struggle to find the line between the character and the fact that it's John Cusack playing the character.

Despite the lens through which a lot of people view Rob changing, it doesn't change the fact that *High Fidelity* still holds its own as a cult classic to this day.

12

High Fidelity, the Musical?

The conceit of a *High Fidelity* musical is one of those things, that when you first think about it, seems like a joke. With the exception of Barry or Marie, these characters don't necessarily seem like the type to launch into song. In the case of Barry, when he eventually does launch into song at the end, it certainly wouldn't be the type of singing you'd expect to hear on the Great White Way. A *High Fidelity* musical initially seems to be the sort of thing that the guys in the record store would mock.

But the more you think about it, the more you think about the fact that it actually *does* lend itself to being onstage, just not in your traditional way. While Barry is the only character we see singing in the film, music is the absolute soul that brings *High Fidelity* to life. Without music, there is no *High Fidelity*. So with the right team assembled, yes, you could definitely find a way to bring credence to a musical adaptation.

Plus, when you're in the theater, it's even easier to get away with having a character talk directly to the audience. While there was debate when the film was being made over whether or not they could get away with direct address, you don't have that problem in a musical. It would not only be perfectly acceptable to have Rob addressing the audience as the narrator in a musical, it might also be expected to a certain extent.

The other thing is, of course, the setting. Once you accept that there is going to be a musical adaptation, all you need to do is close your eyes and imagine the record store coming to life before your very eyes. That is enough to get anyone excited—as long as it's done right. Much like how it is in the film, it can't be a world that is *too* colorful. It needs to be bland and desolate. It has to be beautiful, but in a way that drives people away, as opposed to bringing people in.

Having a central location, like a record store, also lends itself to being on the stage. Plus, what you can do with fantasy sequences is pretty limitless onstage. The more you think about it, weighing the pros and the cons, the more you realize maybe this *could* work.

The genesis for the musical truly began, however, long before the movie started production.

It all started with the musical's composer Tom Kitt. In the mid-1990s, Kitt was in his early twenties and fresh out of high school. When he went home for Thanksgiving one year, he paid a visit to his high school English teacher, Jock Montgomery. While visiting Jock, Kitt asked him to recommend books that he might not be familiar with. One of the books that Montgomery suggested was *High Fidelity*.

This was years before the film came out, and the source material wasn't quite in the mainstream in the United States. Not unlike DeVincentis, Cusack, Pink, and even Scott Rosenberg, Kitt found many different elements in the book that he could relate to. For starters, he was a record collector whose life was also more or less controlled by pop music. There was just so much in the book that personally spoke to Kitt, so much so that he stored a lot of it away in the back of his mind.

"I had gotten into the BMI Theater Workshop with Brian Yorkey, my collaborator," Kitt recalls about how the initial idea of turning *High Fidelity* into a musical came to be.

I remember our teacher said that we should be on the lookout for things that really speak to us and we feel like fit out voice that we kind of see an opportunity to create a musical where other people might not.

I just thought, *If you could create a musical about love and music and set it to an original score, kind of a soundtrack that draws on all of these styles, you could have something really thrilling and meaningful.* For me, it was something I felt like I could step into and create something new for the theater.[1]

At that point, Kitt wasn't even sure just how popular the book was. In the days that predated social media, it was harder to keep track of that sort of thing. Sure, the Internet existed in the 1990s. But the only way to find out if there were other likeminded fans of something would be via a fan site or perhaps even a message board.

Around that same time, Kitt met Amanda Green at BMI. The world of theater was in Green's blood, as her mother was the actress and singer Phyllis Newman, while her father was the lyricist and playwright Adolph Green. At the time, Green was performing her cabaret shows all around New York. Kitt was taken with her hilarious and witty song lyrics, so he pitched her *High Fidelity*. She enjoyed the source material and jumped on board.

The next step was making sure that the rights to the musical could be secured. For any creative, there's nothing worse than pouring your heart and soul into a project just to be told that you won't be allowed to proceed with it. So before they got too far, Kitt and Green set out to see who had the rights.

Because Touchstone made the film adaptation, they also had the rights for the musical. Kitt and Green wrote some songs and presented them to Disney. The songs were well received, and permission was granted. So now they could properly continue with *High Fidelity* the musical.

At this point, Kitt and Green started dipping their toes in the water by trying out some of the songs in New York cabaret shows. Some of the earliest songs they tried out includes Marie's solo, "Ready to Settle" as well as Barry's big turning point at the end of the show, "Turn the World Off, Turn You On." They also enlisted friend Mario Cantone to do a spot-on Bruce Springsteen impression and wrote a duet for Rob and the Bruce Springsteen that lives in his head to do together, "Goodbye and Good Luck."

"All of these songs got such a great response when we'd perform them," says Kitt. "So we felt like we had this core group of songs that we could really build the musical around."[2]

These cabaret shows that Kitt and Green were doing started to generate some buzz around New York. The shows more or less even served as pseudo–backers auditions, which is where you'd perform the show for potential investors.

So they gathered a variety of their talented friends—some of whom, like Jen Colella who read Laura, wound up in the actual Broadway production. Given the response to these shows, it seemed the songs and the material they were creating were really resonating with audiences.

As the shows were picking up traction, they caught the attention of producers Jeffrey Seller, Robyn Goodman, and Kevin McCollum. These producers were like a dream team when it came to getting a show produced in New York. Seller and McCollum had discovered Jonathan Larson in the early 1990s and wound up producing *Rent* off-Broadway before it went to Broadway in 1996.

The team of Seller, Goodman, and McCollum were also fresh off the heels of another unconventional musical project, *Avenue Q*. *Avenue Q* was an adult take on *Sesame Street* using puppets to depict the real life struggles of adulthood including losing your job, one-night stands, racism, pornography, and pretty much every taboo you could think of. *Avenue Q* started off-Broadway before moving to Broadway and also winning best musical.

The trio wound up loving what they were hearing and immediately expressed interest in working with Kitt and Green on the show. This made perfect sense. Given their track record, Seller, Goodman, and McCollum clearly had an eye for turning rather unconventional and more adult projects into Tony-winning gold. So with the right producers on board, it was time to think about what the next steps were.

To help transition *High Fidelity* from just a couple of really good songs to a full-fledged musical, a solid creative team was assembled.

David Lindsay-Abaire came on board to write the book for the show. Lindsay-Abaire had a long list of theater credits leading up to *High Fidelity* that included the off-Broadway and regional plays *A Devil Inside*; *Fuddy Meers*; *Snow Angel*; *Kimberly Akimbo*; and *Wonder of the World*. The same year that *High Fidelity* opened, he had his first Broadway show, *Rabbit Hole*, open to critical acclaim and even garner him a Pulitzer Prize. *High Fidelity*, however, was his first musical.

To direct the show, the creative team enlisted Walter Bobbie. Bobbie had started his career as a performer having been in productions of *Grease*; *Going Up*; and the 1992 revival of *Guys and Dolls*. As a director, he was perhaps best known at that point for directing the iconic 1996 revival of *Chicago*, for which he won a Tony Award for Best Director, as well as the 2005 revival of *Sweet Charity*.

With a team that had that many accomplishments under their belt, who wouldn't take that bet? Everything seemed aligned for *High Fidelity* to work as a stage musical, just as it had as a movie.

Early on, one of the first things that Bobbie did was help the team hone their script. In some of the earliest drafts, act one was clocking in at an unreasonable two hours. That's a hefty amount of time to expect any audience to stay in their seats without an intermission.

Between Lindsay-Abaire, Bobbie, Kitt, and Green, they brought the script down to a much more sensible running time.

In the fall of 2005, they held their first official reading. The production seemed to have pretty good momentum on its side, as well as producers who believed very passionately in the work that they were seeing. By the following year, the show would be mounted for its official pre-Broadway tryout in Boston. In the theater world, a turnaround time like that from a first reading to a pre-Broadway tryout of a brand new musical is almost unheard of.

Again, one of the most integral things in order for *High Fidelity* to work as a musical boils down to who plays Rob. As in the book and the film, Rob is nothing if not a complicated character. They needed to find someone who exuded the same sort of natural charm that Cusack had in the film, while also being able to sing, dance, and act. That's a lot of boxes that needed to be checked off just in order for the audience to stick with the character.

Will Chase, thankfully, checked off all of those boxes. By the time *High Fidelity* rolled around, Chase was an accomplished theater actor, having appeared in *Rent*; *Miss Saigon*; *Lennon*; *Aida*; and *The Full Monty*, which is where Kitt first saw him.

"You felt like he could be that wonderful combination of someone that you root for," says Kitt, "despite all of their shortcomings and the pretty bad things that they do."[3]

Jen Colella returned to the material to play Laura, with Jay Klaitz as Barry, Christian Anderson as Dick, and Emily Swallow as Marie.

The show started previews of its pre-Broadway run at the Colonial Theater in Boston on September 26 with opening night on October 5. The creative team was riding the wave of the buzz-filled cabaret shows and the successful reading. Everything seemed poised to go.

"It felt like we were really discovering the show," recalls Kitt. "Audiences were great. We were celebrating on opening night. We were so proud. I think the local TV reviews were coming in and they were really positive and we were feeling great."⁴

That feeling of greatness, sadly, didn't last as long as anyone would have wished. By the time everyone woke up the following morning, negative reviews were in the Boston papers. For the first time since the adventure started, there were potholes.

The reviews were none too kind. One universal critique was in regard to Rob and Laura's relationship, which many noted felt like it was a mere secondary plot, despite so much of Rob's life hinging on it. Noted a review in the online publication *Talkin' Broadway*,

> Laura is relegated to a bland, reactive supporting role that involves her taking up with a spiritualist named Ian (Jeb Brown), but doesn't define her role as the lynchpin of Rob's existence.⁵

Says Kitt,

> I think a day or two after, the *Variety* review came out, and that was a really positive one. So we kind of felt *Okay. There's someone who gets the show.* That gave us some confidence. But it was shaky coming out of Boston, obviously. It just felt like that kind of confidence in the material and what we were doing had been shaken.⁶

While to most this might seem like a massive red flag, this is actually all part of the process of going out of town with a Broadway-bound show. You want to be able to see what doesn't work before you reach your final destination. That way, you'll have a chance to make all the tweaks and adjustments needed to produce a tighter and stronger show. For that reason alone, the harsher reviews were actually beneficial.

With that, the team rolled up their sleeves and got to work. One of the first things to go was a song they had written to be an intentionally syrupy love song, "Wonderful Love." This was a song that Barry played in the record store, ironically, just to torture everyone and lament about how terrible it was, just as he would with "I Just Called to Say I Love You." Somewhere down the line, the song wound up getting repurposed as a connection song for Rob and Laura. Unsurprisingly, it didn't quite work once it was taken out of its initial context.

This was replaced by a song, "Laura, Laura," that had more of a Ben Folds–type vibe to it.

"Ben Folds is one of those brilliant writers who can write love songs," says Kitt, "but they have a tension to them and an edge to them. He has this way of saying 'I love you' but it's wrapped in this beautiful vulnerability."[7]

The show also saw the addition of a character from the book, Johnny the Drunk, now dubbed the Most Pathetic Man in the World. With some additional tweaks to the show's book, score, and choreography, the team felt like they were ready to conquer Broadway.

The show had its first preview on November 20, less than a month after the show had wrapped its Boston run on October 22. That's a lot of change to implement, but everyone seemed confident that they had done the work that needed to be done. That confidence was further demonstrated by the audience reaction, which Kitt compared to being at a rock concert.

> You're sitting in this full house of people who are really appreciating what you did. One of our producers kind of spoke to it afterwards, how great that felt. And I just remember being on cloud nine.[8]

Opening night rolled around, Thursday, December 7. While nerves were certainly present given the critical reaction the show had received in Boston, this was overshadowed by a sense of excitement. In the crowd for opening night was Hornby, who was getting to see characters he had conceived eleven years before brought to life in a brand new way he hadn't fathomed when he wrote the book.

When first approached to give the musical his blessing, Hornby didn't need any convincing.

"I never thought of this happening," Hornby remembers thinking at the time, "but I really like these people. And if they think they can do it, then they should do it."[9]

"I know for any writer, that kind of thing, it's very personal," says Kitt. "You let it out into the world in this way, and it felt like an honor for Nick Hornby to give us permission to take this beloved material and adapt it for the stage."[10]

The process of a Broadway opening night was a new experience for both Kitt and Green as writers. In the pre-Internet review days, how it worked was you had the party and essentially waited for the newspapers to hit the newsstands the next morning. You'd only get a sense of just how your show'd been received in the early hours of the morning, while you were on the edge of your seat waiting for the ink to dry. Now that the digital age had rolled around, as soon as the curtain comes down, you know exactly what they think.

Ben Brantley of the *New York Times* was none too keen on the show. His main takeaway from *High Fidelity* was simply how much of it he couldn't remember. He used the source material's own storytelling device against the show by dubbing it one of his own Broadway's top five "all-time forgettable musicals."[11]

"Here composer Tom Kitt emerges with a copycat, reverential, referential pastiche," wrote Clive Barnes for the *New York Post*. "It might have worked had it had the spectral vitality of Jonathan Larson's "Rent." But Kitt's music offers the fatal combination of sounding familiar yet unmemorable."[12]

These reviews are hardly glowing endorsements. What started out as a fun and festive night quickly turned into something a lot more depressing. With reviews like those, how could you not be emotionally drained of all that energy you had coming off the stage?

The question quickly became "What next?" There have been many shows that have been deemed more or less critic proof. Some shows can exceed expectations and really strike a chord with audiences, critics be damned. People forget that shows like *Wicked* had luke-warm reviews from critics. Could the same be said for *High Fidelity*?

"I got a sense going into it that we needed a boost with tickets," says Kitt.

> So now you start to fear about the show's ability to run. And of course, those fears were quite founded. We opened Thursday, December 6. I feel like the following Monday, we were called in to the office with Jeffrey, Kevin, and Robyn and they gave us the news that they were going to have to close the show the following weekend.[13]

By all accounts, it was devastating for everyone involved. On December 17, less than two weeks after the show opened on Broadway, the cast took its final bow.

Like anything else, it all came down to money. Ticket sales were far below what had been expected. Not to mention that January through March are traditionally slow months for the theater because let's face it, who the hell wants to go out to do stuff during a harsh New York winter?

It also didn't help that *High Fidelity* bit off more than it could chew in regard to theater choice. A show so rough around the edges got absolutely swallowed up at the Imperial Theater, which seats 1,417. That seating puts the Imperial among the larger Broadway theaters.

The show would've been much more at home at a smaller theater, like perhaps the Hayes, which seats 597.

One thing the show did have going for it was the cast album. From the jump, the producers knew that no matter what happened, they needed to record the cast album. Without an album, your show will never have a life outside that moment. Despite the show losing its investment, the producers were true to their word. In early 2007, they recorded the official cast album.

The tactic worked. Since 2006, the show has taken on a new life in regional theaters and community theaters throughout the world. The show has shown that it has the staying power necessary to carry the torch long after *High Fidelity* left New York.

"I believe in this musical the way I did back in the mid-'90s when I first thought of the idea," says Kitt. "And I'm excited for the life of *High Fidelity* as a musical and what could be next."

To quote the show's opening number, Kitt adds, "I wouldn't change a thing about it."[14]

13

Hulu's *High Fidelity*

"One of the things in *High Fidelity* is it's very much a male-oriented story, I think," says Simmons. "And it's very much a male-oriented story of a certain age. I wonder if you made *High Fidelity* today, I wonder what changes you would make. And maybe you couldn't. Maybe you couldn't make it today."[1]

Well, in fact, that is exactly what they wound up doing, twenty years after the film came out and twenty-five years after the book came out. Enough time had gone by without a new iteration of Rob and the gang from Championship Vinyl. We were due for another visit.

In an era where everything else is coming back, why shouldn't *High Fidelity*? By the time the Hulu series premiered in 2020, it had already been a book, a movie, and a Broadway musical. It seems like following Rob over the course of a ten-episode series would be the next logical step for the character. On paper, the idea made perfect sense. It could work.

Going back to its inception, the idea for the show came about as a result of creators Veronica West and Sara Kucserka. The pair got their start in television as story editors on *Ugly Betty* before working together on other shows such as *Mercy*; *Brothers & Sisters*; *GCB*; *Hart of Dixie*; *State of Affairs*; *Chicago Fire*; and *Bull*.

"It was a book and a movie that we had both always been obsessed with and always loved," Kucserka said in an interview.

And we hit this point in our career where we had like that come-to-Jesus moment of like, "Are we really writing the shows that we want to be writing?" And we were not. And we sat down and said, "Okay. Dream scenario, what do we want to write?" And the number one thing that we put up on a tiny pink notecard in our office was "*High Fidelity* from a woman's point of view."[2]

At that point, Kucserka and West began trying to get their dream project made. They started pitching it around town, before eventually pitching the idea to a production company, Midnight Radio, founded by Josh Appelbaum, André Nemec, Jeff Pinkner, and, yes, Scott Rosenberg.

Obviously, it is a bizarre twist of fate that, after everything that happened with the arbitration process on the film adaptation, a project like this would wind up in the lap of Scott Rosenberg. How it happened, however, was pretty simple. They were looking to have someone on the show who had worked on the film. Kucserka and West got a call from their agent saying a meeting'd been set up with Rosenberg and Midnight Radio.

Everyone at Midnight Radio loved the idea. When it was first pitched, the series was to feature a female lead and would take place in the L.A. hipster scene that is Silverlake. Just as DeVincentis, Pink, and Cusack had a connection to Chicago, Kucserka and West had their own personal connection to Silverlake so that is where they wanted to set the series.

As it so happened, Midnight Radio had a deal with ABC at the time. ABC is owned by Disney, which also owns Touchstone, and it was Touchstone that made the film *High Fidelity*. So it was all in the family. Not to mention that Hornby had also recently gotten the rights squared away that would make a *High Fidelity* series possible. There were a number of factors that were seemingly working in their favor.

On April 5, 2018, *Deadline* announced the series. At the time, it was picked up by a then-nameless Disney streaming service that would later become Disney+.[3]

The next question became what would happen with the Rob character? When the series was picked up, it had been a mere six months since the allegations against Harvey Weinstein had come out, which saw the beginning of the #MeToo movement.

As a result, during this time we as a culture started looking at everything from the past through a new lens, and in many cases rightfully so. What may have been deemed acceptable—or at the very least had been carelessly overlooked—was no longer overlooked or found acceptable. So it seemed the idea of expecting audiences to sympathize with a man like Rob, who in many ways could be characterized as problematic, would be an uphill battle that might be better left unfought in 2020.

Could you make *High Fidelity* in 2020? Certainly. Could you do so with a man? Most likely. But given that think pieces about, as DeVincentis puts it, "how much Rob sucks" existed before 2020, you can imagine there'd be a lot more walking on egg shells that you'd have to do to try to replicate exactly what *High Fidelity* had been twenty years before. The culture had evolved, why shouldn't the story?[4]

So if *High* Fidelity was going to be revived, going the gender swap route seemed like the right way to go. Telling the story through a different prism would also be further proof that the story was totally universal. Just as it wasn't about London or Chicago, it also wasn't about whether Rob was a man or a woman. This would show people, once and for all, that the true success of *High Fidelity* was the story itself.

Of course, no *High Fidelity* project could take place without getting the seal of approval of Nick Hornby. He approved right away.

"I think the gender flipping is really interesting, because it's just not about who you think it's about, really, with that book," Hornby said right around the time of the show's release. "There's hundreds of people that come up and say, 'It's me.' They're not all the same people. They're not all the same color, and they're not all the same gender."[5]

The other thing that the series had going for it was the timing. When the book was written, more and more record stores were going under. This was, obviously, because people who didn't really care about what format they heard their music in were flocking to their local megastore for compact discs. CDs were in and records were out—much to the dismay of music obsessives everywhere. Certain record stores managed to hang on, of course. But at a certain point, the shift could definitely be felt.

Then about ten years later, the shift happened once again. People started going in an entirely different direction and stopped buying CDs. Now, everything is digital and most people have their entire music library on their phone via Spotify, Pandora, Amazon Music, and all the other music apps.

Of course, if something hangs around long enough, it'll become relevant again. At a certain point, records, or *vinyls* as they are now called, started becoming hip or retro. It happened slowly at first, where you could maybe find a small selection of limited-edition records at a Barnes & Noble or even a Target, for instance.

But eventually, records started becoming popular again. Now there's a brand-new generation of record collectors and music obsessives. Who would have guessed? Of course, there were those who never gave up on records. These were the men and women who were keeping record stores alive when they needed it most: during those in-between years.

Just because records have become commercially viable again doesn't mean that record stores are automatically in the clear, however. Most millennials who collect vinyl aren't going to be seeking out record stores. They'll go to a big box retailer or even a place like Urban Outfitters. Or when all else fails, they'll log on to Amazon and just go the convenience route. For the most part, record shops aren't really their scene.

As a result, it is perfectly logical that Championship Vinyl could still be hanging on by a single thread in this day and age. Of course, being in a more hipster location might help business, as there are still those rare birds who prefer to browse the racks. But by and large, being a record shop owner still wouldn't be considered a thriving or sexy career option.

That's where we find the current landscape of *High Fidelity* for the reboot. Just as in Scott Rosenberg's initial draft of the film, the topic of gentrification played a role in the series. This is because, in the years since the book was written, gentrification became more prominent than it was before. It was a story that many big-city communities could relate to. Now, it was all being told from the perspective of Rob.

The goal of Kucserka and West was to create a character that didn't really fit in to the modern world. This is sort of a requirement when you've got a character who manages a shop that sells physical media during a time when digital media is clearly all the rage. This helped set things up in sort of a fish-out-of-water way. Rob, after all, was never supposed to be the coolest person in the room. We needed to see Rob fail and struggle and also have moments when her, in this case, judgment was not always solid.

When it came to casting, someone suggested Zoe Kravitz. According to Rosenberg, he loved the idea but he felt it was a ridiculous longshot that she'd do it. The casting makes total sense on paper. For starters, she is the daughter of Lenny Kravitz, which earns her automatic credibility in the music world right there. More than that, her mom is Lisa Bonet. So having Zoe would sort of be passing the torch from one *High Fidelity* adaptation to another, keeping it all in the extended family, in a way.[6]

Zoe was sent the script and immediately responded to the material. She loved it. Her only request was that the series be moved from

Silverlake to Brooklyn. Her request was granted. The series moved cross-country, and thus *High Fidelity* had a new star.

"I've lived in New York for fifteen, sixteen years now," Kravitz said in an interview, regarding setting the story there, "and there's just nothing like it."

> When you get to make something that takes place there and really be on that street and have that energy, with the extras and everything? They're amazing, they're local, they live around there. So you're feeding off of that energy. And you can't fake that.[7]

Naturally, the gender swap wasn't limited to just Rob—now named Robyn, or Rob for short. For the character of Barry, now named Cherise, the filmmakers landed on Da'Vine Joy Randolph. After garnering lots of attention for her work in the musical adaptation of *Ghost*, which earned her a Tony Award nomination, Randolph began working steadily in TV and film.

Just a few months before *High Fidelity* was released in 2020, Randolph had a breakout role in Eddie Murphy's *Dolemite Is My Name*. It was a situation not unlike Jack Black's portrayal of Barry in the original movie. After *Dolemite*, Randolph had quite a bit of clout behind her. So while she wasn't entirely well-known when the show was filming, that seemed to have changed by the time we finally saw the show.

For Dick, his name was changed to Simon, but he was still portrayed by a man. This time, it was David H. Holmes. In the series, the character evolved a bit, as he was now not only gay but also one of Rob's illustrious five heartbreaks. Despite the breakup, the pair did still manage to remain friends.

That's a principal theme that remains in the series, of course. We, again, see Rob revisiting her former lovers. However, given the modern-day setting, we can now see Rob as she struggles to get back out there in the dating scene via the dreaded dating apps. It adds a whole new layer to Rob's post–breakup frustration. While we saw Rob in the book and film have a one-night stand, we didn't really see him actively try to get back out there in the dating scene. What happened with Marie was essentially just a glorified hook-up.

When it was first announced that the series would be acquired by Disney+, Disney believed that they were going to be able to push some boundaries in regard to what they could do with their intellectual properties. This is why they greenlit *High Fidelity* as well as other shows like *Love, Simon* and a reboot of *Lizzie McGuire* that would've shown a more mature version of the character in her thirties.

At a certain point, however, the team at Disney+ decided that they wanted to maintain the more family-friendly image that their parent company had built its foundation on. This meant that they had to change the course of action with some of the shows they'd picked up, including *High Fidelity.*

According to Scott Rosenberg, he realized that something was up when he noticed Disney was pushing back on "the most minor stuff." At that point, the team decided they needed to quit. They felt that they had to remain true to the source material, which didn't quite fall into the land of Mickey Mouse. At that point, Disney said, "You know, we also own Hulu."[8]

Over the previous decade, Disney had been acquiring all sorts of other companies. It started when Disney bought Marvel Entertainment in 2009. This was followed by Lucas Films and eventually 20th Century Fox. When Disney acquired Fox, they also got a 60 percent stake in Hulu.

This allowed Disney to spread its intellectual property around and not feel like everything Disney did had to be boxed into a clean-cut image.

With the show now in place, it was picked up for a ten-episode order. Initial reaction to the fact that they were adapting *High Fidelity* for TV was mixed. The Internet is, of course, what the Internet is. Whenever a remake or reboot of anything is announced, it doesn't matter what property it is. There will be backlash, misplaced anger, and laments of *Why has Hollywood run out of original ideas?* Sprinkled in the midst of these will be a smattering of *Hey, this could be good.*

One person who was not on board from the jump, or at the very least was skeptical, was John Cusack.

> They want to brand their thing with our thing—they'll fuck it up . . . The woman part seems good/the rest not so much—but it's Nick's book [I] hope at least he's involved—if he's not—it'll suck.[9]

There was, of course, lots of discussion about what type of music would be featured in the series. Just as it was integral to get the music for the film just right, the team behind the series was as determined to find the same sense of authenticity for the series.

To accomplish what they were trying to do, they sought out the help of Aperture Music, a music supervision and editing company made up of industry vets Manish Raval, Tom Wolfe, and Alison Rosenfeld.

Aperture Music has a pretty solid résumé in the film and TV markets, boasting credits that include *Green Book*; *Trainwreck*; *Girls*; *Black Monday*; *The Boys*; *Preacher*; *New Girl*; and *Donnie Darko*.

Aperture was brought on by West and Kucserka before Kravitz was on board and while the show was still set in Los Angeles. Once the series made the jump to Crown Heights, that of course impacted the type of music Rob would be listening to. Kravitz was also very involved in the show's soundtrack.

When you're doing anything for film or television that requires an insane amount of well-recognized music, it's almost guaranteed that clearance issues will come up at some point. It's a similar hurdle that the team who made the movie encountered. Just because you've got your heart set on using something doesn't mean you'll necessarily be able to. You might think you're on the right track with something, and then you're thrown entirely off track by something out of your control. That's why there always needs to be a lot of flexibility when you're trying to make something. The Hulu series was no different.

What worked its way into the show, however, is definitely noteworthy. Some of the biggest standouts were Fleetwood Mac; Marvin Gaye; Frank Zappa; David Bowie; Ann Peebles; Outkast; Prince; Blondie; Beastie Boys; Aretha Franklin; the Grateful Dead; Jimi Hendrix; the Replacements; Ike and Tina Turner; Cheap Trick; Dead Kennedys; the Beta Band; the Roots; Frank Ocean; Janet Jackson; Ted Lucas; and Darando.[10]

Even Nick Drake, whom the team for the film had tried to get for their soundtrack, wound up in the series. Lenny Kravitz did *not* have a song in the series, probably because that would be a bit too on the nose.

The series had a handful of different directors, including Natasha Lyonne, Jeffrey Reiner, Andrew DeYoung, Chioke Nassor, and Jesse Peretz. The latter actually just so happened to be a close friend of Seamus McGarvey. McGarvey expressed interest in working on the series initially. "I lived in his flat in New York City for three years after my divorce," recalls McGarvey. "And I actually rang him up and said, 'I will shoot this.' And he said, 'No, no. *High Fidelity* looked shit.'"[11]

Three people who have no credited involvement with the show are John Cusack, D.V. DeVincentis, and Steve Pink. That being said, despite not being credited, their work still manages to exist on the screen when you watch the show.

The series is credited as being an adaptation of the book, not the movie. However, DeVincentis and Pink couldn't help but notice their own work represented on the show—specific things that they personally brought to the script. All of this was done without any permission or credit given.

This could have been a direct result of the fact that because Scott Rosenberg was involved and the creators thought they had permission to use dialogue from the film. Of course, Rosenberg's dialogue never actually wound up in the film, while DeVincentis, Pink, and Cusack didn't actually own any rights to the material created for the film.

"I didn't see the TV show," says DeVincentis of the series.

> I read the pilot, and I was kind of stunned to find our writing in their script. Like, a lot of it. Just lifted from the screenplay of the movie and dropped down into the TV show. I'd never seen anything like it. The TV show was supposedly an adaptation of the book, not an adaptation of the movie—that's what the credits say. Yet there were entire scenes, concepts, shots, and dialog lifted directly from the movie—again *not* from the book—without any credit or attribution.[12]

"The problem is that it is a remake of our movie," says Pink.

> It's not not a remake. You can't look at the TV show and look at our movie and fucking think that the TV show was not a remake. I don't know how with an honest face you could make that determination.[13]

In the film, there's an inside joke that DeVincentis wrote into the script, a joke that was just between himself and a high school friend. Naturally, the reference was lifted directly from the film and brought into the script.

It wasn't just dialogue that was written into the film's script, either. During the scene in the movie where Barry is antagonizing Rob in the record store and they get into a brief physical altercation, a worried Dick sits on the counter, and meekly says, "Break it up." This was a Todd Louiso adlib, the idea that Dick was telling them to stop it but clearly had no intention of jumping in or getting involved. This was not scripted and yet, there it was on TV.

"It was kind of retraumatizing after what we went through twenty years ago with Rosenberg, again someone putting their name on *your* passion, on something *you* toiled to create," says DeVincentis.[14]

The next step, it seemed, would be for DeVincentis and Pink to go to the WGA for arbitration and credit. If it worked for Scott Rosenberg, it should work for them, right? But that's not exactly how it works.

In order for DeVincentis and Pink to arbitrate and to make their case to the WGA, the WGA first had to determine whether or not the new series was a remake of the film. Until the property was considered a remake or a reboot, DeVincentis and Pink would not be able to make their case.

Ultimately, the WGA decided that the series was not a remake of the film, but rather an adaptation of the book. Therefore, DeVincentis and Pink couldn't prove they deserved credit for, yes, the many lines of dialogue that had been directly lifted from the film that they wrote.

Says Pink,

> There is no way to determine whether D.V. and I and Johnny would've gotten credit. We could've been considered a remake, we could've written a defense trying to sway the arbitrators that our work is represented in the new work and therefore we deserve credit on the TV show. But we'll never know.[15]

While Scott Rosenberg admits that the idea of having Zoe Kravitz as Rob directly address the camera was 100 percent lifted from the film, he points out that the movie is owned by Disney, and it was Disney that gave them the money to do the series. Therefore, they were free to do "whatever the hell we wanted."

> We certainly wouldn't have given them a credit and let them be part of the process. I don't need to ever speak to those guys again. So I'm not gonna go, "Hey, come in my writers room, fellas!"[16]

"I'm flattered by their desire to embrace our work, and I don't even necessarily blame them," Pink adds.

> They could've ripped us off all they want, we don't own the material. Disney owns the material. We don't own the book. Nick Hornby wrote the book. Not only did we not write the underlining material, we don't own the material we wrote. So it's only about whether or not we would be afforded credit of our work inside all of that.[17]

Ultimately DeVincentis and Pink didn't receive any credit on the series. The series was credited as being "based on a book by Nick Hornby."

"I don't really want to comment on the way it was credited because I honestly didn't have anything to do with how that was determined," Veronica West said when the subject came up in an interview.

> It's one of my top five films of all time for sure, if not the top. And it was just a longtime dream of mine to be able to remake this property because it seemed like there was so much potential to tell a fresh story that's still, at the same time, true to the qualities that are so enduring about the movie and this book.[18]

On February 14, 2020, the series premiered on Hulu. The general reaction to the series was positive, and it garnered an impressive 86 percent Fresh on Rotten Tomatoes: "Though it skips the occasional beat, *High Fidelity*'s fresh take on a familiar track is as witty as it is emotionally charged, giving a curmudgeonly charming Zoë Kravitz plenty of room to shine," Rotten Tomatoes wrote as part of their critical consensus. The cast was universally praised, with many reviewers signaling out both Kravitz as well as Da'Vine Joy Randolph. They felt that the series was a love letter to the source material, which when you watch it, is something you cannot help but pick up on. That being said, you also get the sense that it was just as much a homage to the movie as it was the novel.[19]

Still, the praise for the series wasn't entirely universal. There were many critics and audience members who felt the show was "purposeless" and who couldn't quite find a convincing argument within the series for why it deserved to exist. A popular sentiment on social media at that time from those critics was simply "Who is this show for?" Then of course, in the age of a certain section of the public taking umbrage with a female *Ghostbusters*, others on social media were quick to write the gender swap off as being "woke."

Hornby did his best before the show's release to try to discourage that type of criticism. He wrote an op-ed for *Rolling Stone* at the time in which he defended the series, saying he was totally in support of the direction they were taking things.

"*High Fidelity* the TV show deals with the world we're in now," Hornby wrote.

> The playlists are made digitally, yet the hearts that are broken by feckless men and women are still inconveniently and painfully analog. Somehow, Rob survived the move into the twenty-first century because people are still willing to pay for something that's as ubiquitous as the air we breathe. After I began to use

Spotify, I thought, "This is incredible: every piece of music I'll ever need, in a small box in my pocket."[20]

"I couldn't be more proud of the show," Hornby concluded the article by saying,

> And if I catch anyone saying it's self-consciously "woke," what with its gender reversals and its inclusion of more than one race/sexuality, I will come 'round to your house and put you back to sleep. Because, guess what: *High Fidelity* isn't just about you. It's about people who *aren't* like you, too.

Despite the advanced defense from Hornby, sadly, it didn't make much of a difference in the grand scheme of things. While many discovered the show during the pandemic in March, this was not enough to have it picked up for a second season.

On August 5, 2020, Hulu announced that the series had been canceled after just one season. According to *Deadline*, there were lots of discussions going on within Hulu in the days leading up to this with "internal support" from some of the Hulu brass.

The fact that there was internal support does make sense. The show was very well-received critically. Plus, there's also the fact that Kravitz was already a star on the rise when the show was canceled. So having people on the inside vying to bring the show back for a second season wouldn't be out of the realm of possibility.

An official reason for the cancellation was never given. Since Hulu doesn't release ratings, we also have no way of knowing just how well or poorly the show did. So for the time being, exactly why the show was canceled remains a mystery.

The reaction of those involved was genuine surprise that the show hadn't been renewed for another season. Rosenberg says there was a lot more they felt they could say in the series.

Said Ben-Adir in an interview,

> Annoyingly, season 2 was really gonna be a Cherise-focused season. She was gonna become the lead of the show, and the story was leaning toward being about where she'd come from, her heartbreaks and her family background.[21]

At the time of the cancellation, Kravitz took to Instagram to express her sadness about the show ending and also took the opportunity to throw a little bit of shade at Hulu. "It's cool. At least hulu has a ton of other shows starring women of color we can watch. Oh wait," she wrote.[22]

In February 2022, two years after the show had premiered, she elaborated on just why she believed Hulu had been so quick to cancel the show. "They didn't realize what that show was and what it could do," Kravitz said in an interview with *Elle*. "The amount of letters, DMs, people on the street, and women that look like us—like, that love for the show, it meant something to people. It was a big mistake."[23]

With that, the chapter on the series was closed. And for now, this also marks the end of what started as a book before coming a movie that became a Broadway musical and finally became a TV series. Given that track record, as well as the material's overall staying power, something tells me we'll be seeing more of Rob, Laura, Barry, Dick, and everyone else in some type of iteration.

After all, one more adaptation and then we'll be able to finally rank the top five definitive incarnations of *High Fidelity*.

Afterword

When you've got something that's as wildly successful and revered as *High Fidelity* is, it leaves people wanting more. Granted, once they get more, they will say that the follow up they were clamoring for was not as good as the original. It happens every time something is a success and it's decided that you need to cash in on that success. There's almost always a little bit—or a lot—of backlash the second time around. It's the classic tale of how quickly they forget just how badly they wanted more and to see where these characters would go.

As for Hornby, he didn't know what that would be. For years, people had been asking him if there'd be a sequel to *High Fidelity*, at least in book form, but he just didn't know where he'd put the characters of the sequel.

"I couldn't figure out what Rob would've ended up doing," he says. "I don't know what those guys did end up doing when the record store started to disappear. Now it's coming back and I can see those guys again. But I don't know what happened to the original generation."[1]

Over the course of my working on this book, there was one thing that stood out more than anything else. No matter how many years have gone by or how our culture has shifted or how many think pieces have been written about why the character Rob is such an asshole, people still have a strong, passionate love for the film.

While the Hulu series may have only lasted a single season, it did prove that there was still enough of an interest in the property for it to be greenlit in the first place. People still strongly identify with these characters. There's a real fondness for just how authentic they are in how they hold up a mirror to who we all are as people, whether we openly admit it or not. The fact remains that so many people are still discovering the book, the movie, the musical, or the series for the first time. That's rarified air right there.

"It did have an edge; a bone-on-bone truth about it," Cusack said about making the film. "The idea of trying to get that movie made now, from a big studio, I just don't think it'd happen. We were getting away with it for different reasons, but mainly we didn't have to sanitize it. It was a different era in the film business."[2]

"I didn't know how rare an experience this was going to be," says Pink about how he looks back on the film.

> I thought we'd just be able to continue to conjure up that kind of stuff and to do it. Everyone who came together, all the artists who came together, filmmakers who came together to make that film. It's cliché, but it was one of those moments in time where everything converged to create this very good film and an amazing experience.[3]

The reach of *High Fidelity* is pretty large, possibly because it is so multifaceted. Yes, it's about a guy who has commitment issues and is going through a thirty-year-old's crisis as he reevaluates his life and what it all means loudly enough for those around him to bear witness to it. Yes, it's a love story at its core. That's actually the angle that attracted Stephen Frears to the project. Ask Stephen Frears what *High Fidelity* is to him, and he will tell you it's just a love story. An unconventional love story, sure. But a love story all the same. Plus, yes, it's also about really great music.

Because there're so many of those working parts to it, there seems to be a little something for everyone. People can relate to it because they are Rob or because they know somebody like Rob. They might be a music obsessive; or someone with commitment issues; or someone who's trying to figure out what it all means; or someone trying to understand why they're the source of all their past relationships falling apart; and so forth.

Even over twenty years later, the film also manages to maintain a special place in the hearts of the people who made it too.

"This is totally one from the heart," says DeVincentis. "I was and still am totally connected to this movie, and it changed my life. I still have people in my life who came from it as well."[4]

One thing that has changed since the book was released in 1995 is how we consume our music. Yes, the immediacy of being able to listen to what you want exactly when you want it without so much as having to wait thirty seconds has also become embedded in our culture.

"You can be looking at a review in the newspaper," says Hornby, "and put the record on straight away, because you've got Spotify. And of course back then, it was about money. *Do I want to spend money on this thing? I want to know more about it. I will read this review.* And you don't need to anymore."[5]

Then there's the return in popularity of records and record collecting as a whole. However, the resurgence of record stores isn't the only thing that's changed in the years since the movie came out. The movie also serves as a time capsule, of sorts, for a version of Chicago—or Wicker Park, more specifically—that has ceased to exist. Oddly enough, there were actually signs of this happening between the time of production wrapping in July 1999 and the film's release in March 2000.

On January 15, 2000, the doors closed for good on Lounge Ax after it'd been an essential part of the Chicago indie music scene for thirteen years. The last band to headline was the Coctails, who had broken up five years earlier but reunited just for this final show at Lounge Ax. So even by the time that audiences were seeing the music scene of Wicker Park immortalized on the big screen, things were already changing.

Like it or not, Wicker Park was on the cusp of becoming gentrified. Slowly but surely, as the years have gone on, more and more locations from the film have slowly morphed as have the surroundings as a whole.

The Double Door held on for as long as it could and managed to stay open significantly longer than many expected it to. There had been talk starting in 2016 that Double Door could be moving to a new location. However, in 2017 the venue was abruptly closed due to eviction.

Then, only a year later, we began hearing whispers that Double Door could be returning after all in a new venue. However, we wouldn't get official confirmation until 2021 when it was announced that they'd be relocating a mile from the original location, moving into the Wilson Theater building. This was a space that had first opened in 1908 and, as of late 2022, was in the process of being renovated with an eye toward opening back up in 2023.[6]

To anyone who lived there during the time when *High Fidelity* was set or even seven years earlier when DeVincentis, Pink, and Cusack still lived in Chicago, the change is noticeable. Yes, it's typical for things to change over the course of twenty to thirty years. But you can't escape the feeling of just how gentrified everything has become.

While many purists may say that you're losing history, which you definitely are when you make some of these changes, there's also the flip side of that coin. There are those who can respect and remember the past while also appreciating the future.

"It's nice to see that the spirit of all that stuff lives on," says Armisen, with perhaps a more optimistic approach to how things have evolved in the time since he lived in Wicker Park. "Physically it's nice to see that it's still a productive part. Wicker Park looks really pretty and it's different, but it still looks great. I still like walking around. I like the balance of having a memory and then also appreciating that everything just changes."[7]

As a result of *High Fidelity*, Nick Hornby went through a change with his own career. *High Fidelity* was his first novel and one that was critically well-received and managed to stand the test of time. So naturally, *High Fidelity* served as a way for Nick Hornby to prove himself and what he can do.

In 1998, Hornby published his second novel, *About a Boy*. Seeing as how his third book was also adapted into a film in 2002 that starred Hugh Grant and Nicholas Hoult, this served as a trifecta that most authors can only dream of: writing material so strong that people wanted to adapt it to other mediums. That is certainly rarified air that Hornby was breathing.

He followed this up with the novels *How to Be Good*; *A Long Way Down*; *Slam*; *Juliet*; *Naked*; *Funny Girl*; *State of the Union*; and *Just Like You*. He's also published nonfiction and even screenplays. While Hornby won't adapt his own written material for the screen, he has no qualms about adapting other people's materials, which he did with the films *An Education*; *Wild*; and *Brooklyn*.

Still, no matter how much Hornby has accomplished in the years that pass, his fondness for *High Fidelity* remains as powerful as ever.

"I'm still proud of it," Hornby says. "I mean, it was a life changer in a lot of ways. It was a first novel and once I had done it, I thought *Oh, I could do more of these.*"

He continues, referencing just how revered the story has become. "I wrote a novel about something I really love, so I really don't mind people talking to me about whatever they want to talk to me about because it continues to be a part of my life. I don't get sick of it."[8]

Acknowledgments

Among those who worked on the film, everyone can agree upon one thing: it was a total labor of love. When working on this book, I can echo that same sentiment. The process of this book, and all of the many rabbit holes I journeyed down in the process, came from a place of passion.

High Fidelity is a story that deeply connects with me in many ways, but mainly in how a love of pop culture can sometimes interfere with one's personal life. So when it came time to write my first book, I knew I had to tell the story of how the film *High Fidelity* got made, its staying power in culture, and the way in which *High Fidelity* has continued to evolve.

Throughout the process of working on the oral history of *High Fidelity* in 2020 for Consequence of Sound—and subsequently this book—the most common thing I encountered with the people who made the movie as well as the musical and the Hulu series was the phrase *This book was made for me*. It all started with the source material. Those who came on board to make the film were fans of the book.

Suffice to say, this book would not exist if not for Nick Hornby. He not only wrote the source material, but he has been gracious with his time for interviews, not to mention supportive of this entire endeavor from day one. I emailed Nick Hornby in January of 2020 to ask him if he'd participate in an oral history on the making of the film *High Fidelity*. Not even two hours later, I received an email reply from Hornby himself that said only, "I'm here. NH."

Nick Hornby was the first one to sign on to participate in the oral history, and when it came time to start working on the book, he was also the first person I interviewed. He has supported my writing this book from day one, and for that I am forever grateful.

Additionally, there are so many more people who came to my rescue to fill in blanks, provide material, and just provide unfathomable degrees of support.

First and foremost, I have to thank two of the film's screenwriters, D.V. DeVincentis and Steve Pink. Both provided countless hours of interviews that were full of insight I would not have had access to otherwise. DeVincentis also provided me with ample documents, scripts, and call sheets. Both DeVincentis and Pink were sources of rich and unparalleled stories that served as the very foundation for this book and upon which I could then build. If not for their support and generosity, this book would be merely a twenty-nine-page pamphlet with little-to-no significance.

I also need to shout out everyone who participated in interviews and whom I would not have been able to accomplish this without: Jack Black, Todd Louiso, Stephen Frears, Seamus McGarvey, Sara Gilbert, Rudd Simmons, Fred Armisen, Victoria Thomas, Mike Newell, Billy Higgins, David Chapman, Mick Audsley, Ben Carr, Tom Kitt, Adam Carston, and Scott Rosenberg.

Then there were those who I initially spoke with for the 2020 oral history for Consequence of Sound including John Cusack, Iben Hjejle, Kathy Nelson, Dan Koretzky, Sara Kucserka, and Veronica West.

I'd also like to thank the entire team at Applause Books, including John Cerullo and Barbara Claire, for recognizing the importance of *High Fidelity* and providing their never-ending support for the entire ride.

Thanks also to my agent, Lee Sobel, for taking a chance and reaching out to a young journalist, expressing interest in maybe turning one of his oral histories into a book. That was in December 2021. By March 2022, I not only had my first agent, but less than four months later I had my very first book deal. Without Lee, this book would be a blank piece of paper.

A big reason why you're holding this book is also due to Michael Roffman, who was the editor at Consequence of Sound I worked with on nine (irresponsibly) expansive oral histories and countless interviews within a short sixteen-month period. Roffman greenlit the *High Fidelity* oral history that started it all with three simple words via email, *Go, Go, Go!* With his enthusiasm, I did just that.

Every young writer needs to have a mentor, and I found one in the incomparable Bill Zehme. When I met Bill, I had written one single article, for which I did not get paid. Today I've got way more experience under my belt, and I even wound up at his old stomping grounds, *Vanity Fair*. There's been not a single person in this industry who's been more supportive of or influential to me than Bill Zehme.

I also have to acknowledge my family, especially my parents Ron and Juli, who spent so many hours of already long days at work indulging my love of film, acting, and theater by taking me to the movies, plays, and auditions. It is that very spirit that lives in this book and all those years of experience that I drew upon.

Lastly, I'd be remiss not to thank everyone else who served as a sounding board, motivator, or even helped me with the occasional lead or bit of inspiration while I was working on the book. I am forever in everyone's debt for cheering me on every step of the way and keeping me from the inevitable internal meltdowns that I was occasionally seemingly on the verge of. I am immensely proud of every comma in this book, and I cannot thank you all enough.

Notes

Chapter 1

1. Nick Hornby, interview by author, 2022.
2. www.theguardian.com/books/2015/nov/01/nick-hornby-brooklyn
-interview.
3. Nick Hornby, interview by author, 2022.
4. Nick Hornby, interview by author, 2022.
5. Nick Hornby, interview by author, 2022.
6. Nick Hornby, interview by author, 2022.
7. www.theguardian.com/books/2015/nov/01/nick-hornby-brooklyn
-interview.
8. https://ew.com/article/1995/09/08/book-review-high-fidelity.
9. www.nytimes.com/1995/09/03/books/a-passion-for-pop.html.
10. Nick Hornby, email to author, 2022.

Chapter 2

1. www.youtube.com/watch?v=g07-IO8agW8.
2. https://catalog.afi.com/Catalog/MovieDetails/53880.
3. Nick Hornby, interview by author, 2022.
4. Scott Rosenberg, interview by author, 2022.
5. Scott Rosenberg, interview by author, 2022.
6. Nick Hornby, interview by author, 2022.

7. Kathy Nelson, interview by author, 2022.
8. www.theguardian.com/theobserver/2001/jul/22/featuresreview.
9. https://consequence.net/2020/04/high-fidelity-oral-history/.
10. Kathy Nelson, interview by author, 2022.
11. D.V. DeVincentis, interview by author, 2022.
12. D.V. DeVincentis, interview by author, 2022.
13. Steve Pink, interview by author, 2022.
14. D.V. DeVincentis, interview by author, 2022.
15. Steve Pink, interview by author, 2022.
16. D.V. DeVincentis, interview by author, 2022.
17. D.V. DeVincentis, interview by author, 2022.
18. Steve Pink, interview by author, 2022.
19. Steve Pink, interview by author, 2022.

Chapter 3

1. Steve Pink, interview by author, 2022.
2. D.V. DeVincentis, interview by author, 2020.
3. https://consequence.net/2020/04/high-fidelity-oral-history/.
4. Nick Hornby, interview by author, 2020.
5. D.V. DeVincentis, interview by author, 2020.
6. Steve Pink, interview by author, 2022.
7. *High Fidelity*, second draft.
8. Steve Pink, interview by author, 2022.
9. D.V. DeVincentis, interview by author, 2020.
10. *High Fidelity*, second draft.
11. *High Fidelity*, second draft.
12. Steve Pink, interview by author, 2022.
13. Nick Hornby, interview by author, 2020.
14. D.V. DeVincentis, interview by author, 2020.
15. Mike Newell, interview by author, 2022.
16. https://consequence.net/2020/04/high-fidelity-oral-history/.
17. Mike Newell, interview by author, 2022.
18. Nick Hornby, interview by author, 2020.

19. Stephen Frears, interview by author, 2020.

20. D.V. DeVincentis, interview by author, 2020.

21. Stephen Frears, interview by author, 2020.

22. D.V. DeVincentis, interview by author, 2020.

23. D.V. DeVincentis, interview by author, 2020.

24. Steve Pink, interview by author, 2022.

25. Steve Pink, interview by author, 2022.

26. Stephen Frears, interview by author, 2020.

27. D.V. DeVincentis, interview by author, 2020.

28. Rudd Simmons, interview by author, 2022.

29. Seamus McGarvey, interview by author, 2022.

30. Seamus McGarvey, interview by author, 2022.

31. Seamus McGarvey, interview by author, 2022.

32. D.V. DeVincentis, interview by author, 2020.

33. Rudd Simmons, interview by author, 2022.

Chapter 4

1. Steve Pink, interview by author, 2022.

2. Billy Higgins, interview by author, 2022.

3. Steve Pink, interview by author, 2022.

4. D.V. DeVincentis, interview by author, 2022.

5. Fred Armisen, interview by author, 2022.

6. Fred Armisen, interview by author, 2022.

7. Billy Higgins, interview by author, 2022.

8. Fred Armisen, interview by author, 2022.

9. Steve Pink, interview by author, 2022.

10. D.V. DeVincentis, interview by author, 2022.

11. D.V. DeVincentis, interview by author, 2022.

12. www.rogerebert.com/roger-ebert/how-mayor-daley-the-first-got-around-his-own-censor-board.

13. Adam Carston, interview by author, 2022.

14. www.chicagotribune.com/entertainment/ct-xpm-2010-06-16-ct-live-0616-blues-brothers-20100616-story.html.

15. Adam Carston, interview by author, 2022.

16. Steve Pink, interview by author, 2022.

17. D.V. DeVincentis, interview by author, 2022.

18. Seamus McGarvey, interview by author, 2022.

19. *High Fidelity*, second draft.

20. Rudd Simmons, interview by author, 2022.

21. David Chapman, interview by author, 2022.

22. D.V. DeVincentis, interview by author, 2022.

23. Dan Koretzky, email to author, 2020.

24. D.V. DeVincentis, interview by author, 2022.

25. Fred Armisen, interview by author, 2022.

26. D.V. DeVincentis, interview by author, 2022.

27. D.V. DeVincentis, interview by author, 2022.

28. Dan Koretzky, email to author, 2020.

29. D.V. DeVincentis, interview by author, 2022.

30. Steve Pink, interview by author, 2022.

31. D.V. DeVincentis, interview by author, 2022.

32. D.V. DeVincentis, interview by author, 2022.

Chapter 5

1. Nick Hornby, interview by author, 2022.

2. Steve Pink, interview by author, 2022.

3. Steve Pink, interview by author, 2022.

4. https://consequence.net/2020/04/high-fidelity-oral-history/.

5. Stephen Frears, interview by author, 2022.

6. Jack Black, interview by author, 2022.

7. Stephen Frears, interview by author, 2022.

8. D.V. DeVincentis, interview by author, 2022.

9. Jack Black, interview by author, 2022.

10. Victoria Thomas, interview by author, 2022.

11. https://consequence.net/2020/04/high-fidelity-oral-history/.

12. Jack Black, interview by author, 2022.

13. Stephen Frears, interview by author, 2022.

14. Jack Black, interview by author, 2022.
15. Stephen Frears, interview by author, 2022.
16. Jack Black, interview by author, 2022.
17. Jack Black, interview by author, 2022.
18. D.V. DeVincentis, interview by author, 2022.
19. Steve Pink, interview by author, 2022.
20. Rudd Simmons, interview by author, 2022.
21. Jack Black, interview by author, 2022.
22. Seamus McGarvey, interview by author, 2022.
23. Jack Black, interview by author, 2022.
24. Todd Louiso, interview by author, 2022.
25. Jack Black, interview by author, 2022.
26. Jack Black, interview by author, 2022.
27. Jack Black, interview by author, 2022.
28. Todd Louiso, text to author, 2022.

Chapter 6

1. D.V. DeVincentis, interview by author, 2022.
2. D.V. DeVincentis, interview by author, 2022.
3. Stephen Frears, interview by author, 2020.
4. Iben Hjejle, interview by author, 2020.
5. Iben Hjejle, interview by author, 2020.
6. Rudd Simmons, interview by author, 2022.
7. D.V. DeVincentis, interview by author, 2022.
8. https://ew.com/movies/high—fidelity—oral—history—john—cusack/.
9. Steve Pink, interview by author, 2020.
10. D.V. DeVincentis, interview by author, 2022.
11. Steve Pink, interview by author, 2020.
12. Victoria Thomas, interview by author, 2022.
13. D.V. DeVincentis, interview by author, 2022.
14. www.youtube.com/watch?v=sPMRl6KV9iU.
15. Billy Higgins, interview by author, 2022.

16. Sara Gilbert, interview by author, 2022.
17. Sara Gilbert, interview by author, 2022.
18. www.youtube.com/watch?v=rS3TtUgEbsM.
19. Ben Carr, interview by author, 2022.
20. D.V. DeVincentis, interview by author, 2020.
21. Steve Pink, interview by author, 2020.

Chapter 7

1. D.V. DeVincentis, interview by author, 2020.
2. Nick Hornby, interview by author, 2020.
3. D.V. DeVincentis, interview by author, 2020.
4. Seamus McGarvey, interview by author, 2022.
5. Seamus McGarvey, interview by author, 2022.
6. Steve Pink, interview by author, 2022.
7. Stephen Frears, interview by author, 2020.
8. Jack Black, interview by author, 2022.
9. Steve Pink, interview by author, 2022.
10. Seamus McGarvey, interview by author, 2022.
11. Stephen Frears, interview by author, 2020.
12. Seamus McGarvey, interview by author, 2022.
13. Billy Higgins, interview by author, 2022.
14. www.nytimes.com/interactive/2020/09/14/magazine/john-cusack -interview.html.
15. D.V. DeVincentis, interview by author, 2020.
16. www.youtube.com/watch?v=sPMRl6KV9iU.
17. Stephen Frears, interview by author, 2020.
18. Rudd Simmons, interview by author, 2022.
19. Billy Higgins, interview by author, 2022.
20. D.V. DeVincentis, interview by author, 2020.
21. D.V. DeVincentis, interview by author, 2020.
22. Steve Pink, interview by author, 2022.
23. D.V. DeVincentis, interview by author, 2020.
24. Jack Black, interview by author, 2022.

25. Sara Gilbert, interview by author, 2022.

26. Steve Pink, interview by author, 2022.

27. D.V. DeVincentis, interview by author, 2020.

28. Jack Black, interview by author, 2022.

29. Iben Hjejle, interview by author, 2020.

30. Seamus McGarvey, interview by author, 2022.

31. Iben Hjejle, interview by author, 2020.

32. Stephen Frears, interview by author, 2020.

33. Steve Pink, interview by author, 2022.

34. Seamus McGarvey, interview by author, 2022.

Chapter 8

1. *High Fidelity*, second draft.

2. *High Fidelity*, shooting script.

3. https://consequence.net/2020/04/high-fidelity-oral-history/.

4. D.V. DeVincentis, interview by author, 2020.

5. Seamus McGarvey, interview by author, 2022.

6. Steve Pink, interview by author, 2020.

7. Steve Pink, interview by author, 2020.

8. Seamus McGarvey, interview by author, 2022.

9. Jack Black, interview by author, 2022.

10. Kathy Nelson, interview by author, 2020.

11. Jack Black, interview by author, 2022.

12. Jack Black, interview by author, 2022.

13. Seamus McGarvey, interview by author, 2022.

14. Stephen Frears, interview by author, 2022.

Chapter 9

1. Rudd Simmons, interview by author, 2022.

2. Mick Audsley, interview by author, 2022.

3. Mick Audsley, interview by author, 2022.

4. Mick Audsley, interview by author, 2022.

5. D.V. DeVincentis, interview by author, 2022.

6. Steve Pink, interview by author, 2022.

7. D.V. DeVincentis, interview by author, 2022.

8. Steve Pink, interview by author, 2022.

9. Mick Audsley, interview by author, 2022.

10. D.V. DeVincentis, interview by author, 2022.

11. Nick Hornby, interview by author, 2022.

12. Mick Audsley, interview by author, 2022.

13. Stephen Frears, interview by author, 2022.

14. Dan Koretzky, email to author, 2020.

15. Steve Pink, interview by author, 2022.

16. D.V. DeVincentis, interview by author, 2022.

17. Mike Newell, interview by author, 2022.

18. Rudd Simmons, interview by author, 2022.

19. D.V. DeVincentis, interview by author, 2022.

20. D.V. DeVincentis, interview by author, 2022.

21. Kathy Nelson, interview by author, 2020.

22. D.V. DeVincentis, interview by author, 2022.

23. Mick Audsley, interview by author, 2022.

24. D.V. DeVincentis, interview by author, 2022.

25. D.V. DeVincentis, interview by author, 2022.

26. D.V. DeVincentis, interview by author, 2022.

27. Mick Audsley, interview by author, 2022.

28. Stephen Frears, interview by author, 2022.

Chapter 10

1. D.V. DeVincentis, interview by author, 2020.

2. www.sxsw.com/wp-content/uploads/2016/08/2000_archive_-_final
.pdf.

3. Steve Pink, interview by author, 2020.

4. D.V. DeVincentis, interview by author, 2020.

5. Scott Rosenberg, interview by author, 2022.

6. D.V. DeVincentis, interview by author, 2020.

7. Scott Rosenberg, interview by author, 2022.

8. Scott Rosenberg, interview by author, 2022.

9. Scott Rosenberg, interview by author, 2022.

10. Steve Pink, interview by author, 2020.

11. Scott Rosenberg, interview by author, 2022.

12. Steve Pink, interview by author, 2020.

13. Steve Pink, interview by author, 2020.

14. D.V. DeVincentis, interview by author, 2020.

15. Scott Rosenberg, interview by author, 2022.

16. D.V. DeVincentis, interview by author, 2020.

17. Scott Rosenberg, interview by author, 2022.

18. Steve Pink, interview by author, 2020.

19. Scott Rosenberg, interview by author, 2022.

Chapter 11

1. www.sxsw.com/wp-content/uploads/2016/08/2000_archive_-_final.pdf.

2. Jack Black, interview by author, 2022.

3. www.rogerebert.com/reviews/high-fidelity-2000.

4. https://archive.nytimes.com/www.nytimes.com/library/film/033100fidelity-film-review.html.

5. www.newsweek.com/breaking-hard-do-157927.

6. www.boxofficemojo.com/date/2000-03-31/.

7. Steve Pink, interview by author, 2022.

8. www.boxofficemojo.com/date/2000-03-31/.

9. Rudd Simmons, interview by author, 2022.

10. Jack Black, interview by author, 2022.

11. www.vice.com/en/article/d35qkw/high-fidelity-created-a-hero-for-a-generation-of-sociopathic-nice-guys.

12. www.theguardian.com/film/2020/mar/31/high-fidelity-john-cusack-nick-hornby.

13. www.nytimes.com/interactive/2020/09/14/magazine/john-cusack-interview.html.

14. D.V. DeVincentis, interview by author, 2022.

15. Steve Pink, interview by author, 2022.

Chapter 12

1. Tom Kitt, interview by author, 2022.

2. Tom Kitt, interview by author, 2022.

3. Tom Kitt, interview by author, 2022.

4. Tom Kitt, interview by author, 2022.

5. www.talkinbroadway.com/page/world/HighFidelity.html.

6. Tom Kitt, interview by author, 2022.

7. Tom Kitt, interview by author, 2022.

8. Tom Kitt, interview by author, 2022.

9. Nick Hornby, interview by author, 2022.

10. Tom Kitt, interview by author, 2022.

11. www.nytimes.com/2006/12/08/theater/reviews/08fide
.html?_r=0andpagewanted=.

12. https://nypost.com/2006/12/08/high-energy-low-fidelity/.

13. Tom Kitt, interview by author, 2022.

14. Tom Kitt, interview by author, 2022.

Chapter 13

1. Rudd Simmons, interview by author, 2022.

2. https://consequence.net/2020/04/high-fidelity-oral-history.

3. https://deadline.com/2018/04/high-fidelity-tv-series-female-lead
-gender-swap-disney-streaming-service-midnight-radio-1202358814/.

4. D.V. DeVincentis, interview by author, 2022.

5. Nick Hornby, interview by author, 2020.

6. Scott Rosenberg, interview by author, 2022.

7. www.indiewire.com/2020/06/zoe-kravitz-high-fidelity-hulu-music
-1202236840/.

8. Scott Rosenberg, interview by author, 2022.

9. www.usatoday.com/story/money/2019/06/03/disney-have
-majority-stake-hulu-after-deal-comcast/1323086001.

10. https://variety.com/2020/artisans/awards/high-fidelity-hulu-music
-1203491510.

11. Seamus McGarvey, interview by author, 2022.

12. D.V. DeVincentis, interview by author, 2022.

13. Steve Pink, interview by author, 2020.

14. D.V. DeVincentis, interview by author, 2022.

15. Steve Pink, interview by author, 2020.

16. Scott Rosenberg, interview by author, 2022.

17. Steve Pink, interview by author, 2022.

18. https://consequence.net/2020/04/high-fidelity-oral-history.

19. www.rottentomatoes.com/tv/high_fidelity/s01.

20. www.rollingstone.com/tv-movies/tv-movie-features/nick-hornby
-on-high-fidelity-reboot-zoe-kravitz-938403/.

21. www.latimes.com/entertainment-arts/tv/story/2020-08-27/kings
ley-ben-adir-barack-obama-malcolm-x-comey-rule-one-night-miami.

22. www.usatoday.com/story/entertainment/tv/2020/08/09/high
-fidelity-star-zoe-kravitz-criticizes-hulu-diversity/3331877001.

23. www.elle.com/culture/celebrities/a39035654/zoe-kravitz
-interview-march-2022.

Afterword

1. Nick Hornby, interview by author, 2022.

2. www.chicagotribune.com/entertainment/ct-ent-john-cusack-talks
-high-fidelity-genesee-theater-0207-story.html.

3. Steve Pink, interview by author, 2020.

4. D.V. DeVincentis, interview by author, 2020.

5. Nick Hornby, interview by author, 2022.

6. https://blockclubchicago.org/2022/11/22/double-door-gets-approval-to-add-marquee-to-new-uptown-home-with-opening-eyed-for-next-year.

7. Fred Armisen, interview by author, 2022.

8. Nick Hornby, interview by author, 2022.

Index

Note: The photo insert images are indexed as *p1*, *p2*, *p3*, etc.

Rob Gordon (character): Carrey as
   possible, 12; at Championship
   Vinyl, 63–64; character flaws
   of, 147–48; Cusack, John, on,
   148; in dating scene, 168–69;
   DeVincentis on, 165; direct
   address by, 95–96, 151; ex
   girlfriends of, 83–84; hang outs
   of, 47; Hornby's development of,
   5–6; Laura's relationship with,
   ix–x, 2, 140, 157; likable nature
   of, 18; motivational speech by,
   108; music collection of, 31;
   narration by, 36; as record store
   owner, x; Top 5 lists of, 29–30
Rock On (underground station), 3
Roger's Park, 28
Rolling Stone magazine, 175
romantic comedies, 146
Roseanne (television), 84
Rosen, Jeff, 109
Rosenberg, Scott, 55, 145; the boys
   calling, 131; Cusack, John,
   friends with, 132; on Disney,
   169; first writer credits sought
   by, 133–35; *High Fidelity* moving
   on by, 13, 129; as *High Fidelity*
   screenwriter, 11–12, 130–35;
   High Fidelity series work of, 164;
   on opening scene, 12–13
Rosenfeld, Alison, 170
Roth, Joe, 14–15, 23–24, 132
Rotten Tomatoes, 139
Rush, 93

Sarah Kendrew (character), 84
Saturday Night Live (television), 126
Say Anything (film), 16, 96, 103–4
scenes: dating, 168–69; energy
   brought to, 91–92; fight, 94;
   Frears cutting, 90; guitar

playing in, 111; indie music,
   44; McGarvey shooting, 93–94;
   not working, 99–100; opening,
   12–13; rain, 98; in record store,
   92; sex, 102–3
School of Rock (film), 145
school teacher, 6
Scorsese, Martin, 17
screenwriters: the boys as, 23–24;
   creatives working as, 29; Cusack,
   John, as, xi, 18; DeVincentis
   as, xi; Hornby as, 11; location
   choice of, 26; music used by,
   60; Pink as, xi; Rosenberg as
   High Fidelity, 11–12, 130–35;
   scripts from, 31; television series
   borrowed from, 172–73
scripts: the boys with draft of, 60–61;
   credit arbitration on, 131–33;
   Cusack, John, and Pink writing,
   22–23; Cusack, John, writing,
   15, 22–23; dialogue heavy, 31;
   draft of, 132–33; failure shown
   in, 60; first writer adaptations
   of, 130; first writer credit for,
   133–35; for *High Fidelity* film,
   35–36; Kravitz, Zoe, sent,
   167–68; Pink writing, 22–23;
   from screenwriters, 31; Wicker
   Park affinity in, 43
Second City, 86
Seller, Jeffrey, 154–55
Serendipity (film), 146
sex scenes, 102–3
shooting: *High Fidelity* film ends,
   104–5; *High Fidelity* film starts,
   89–91
Shore, Howard, 126–27
Sid and Nancy (film), 23
Silverlake (Los Angeles, CA),
   164, 168